FIRST BLACK RED

FIRST BLACK RED

The Story of Chuck Harmon,
the First African American to Play for the Cincinnati Reds

MARTY FORD PIERATT

authorHOUSE®

AuthorHouse™
1663 Liberty Drive
Bloomington, IN 47403
www.authorhouse.com
Phone: 1-800-839-8640

Marty Pieratt
2470 N. State Highway 7
North Vernon, Indiana 47265
1-812-767-8239
martypieratt@yahoo.com
www.martypieratt.com

First published by AuthorHouse 5/3/2010

ISBN: 978-1-4520-2032-7 (e)
ISBN: 978-1-4520-1994-9 (sc)
ISBN: 978-1-4520-1995-6 (hc)

Library of Congress Control Number: 2010906117

Printed in the United States of America
Bloomington, Indiana

This book is printed on acid-free paper.

"Those who deny freedom to others, deserve it not for themselves; and, under a just God, cannot long retain it."

—*President Abraham Lincoln*

"Faith is taking the first step, even when you don't see the whole staircase."

"Let no man pull you low enough to hate him."

"Our lives begin to end the day we become silent about things that matter."

"Man must evolve for all human conflict a method which rejects revenge, aggression, and retaliation. The foundation of such a method is love."

—*Dr. Martin Luther King, Jr.*

"I will never forget that the only reason I'm standing here today is because somebody, somewhere stood up for me when it was risky. Stood up when it was hard. Stood up when it wasn't popular. And because that somebody stood up, a few more stood up. And then a few thousand stood up. And then a few million stood up. And standing up, with courage and clear purpose, they somehow managed to change the world."

—*President Barack Obama.*

"Humankind, and all men ... come from the same source, with the same potentials ... posterity will look back upon what we're doing today in our domestic issue here ... and they'll wonder what the issue was all about. I really think so. It's solved in baseball. It'll be solved in education. It'll be solved everywhere in the course of time."

—Branch Rickey
General Manager, Brooklyn Dodgers, 1943–50.
He signed Jackie Robinson and broke the color barrier in Major League Baseball.

"There's not an American in this country free until every one of us is free.... I'm not as brave as some of these little nine- and ten-year-old kids in the South. I don't like these big teeth that I see on these dogs, and I don't like to see the fierce expressions of the policemen in Birmingham, Alabama. And I don't like to read about pregnant women being poked in the stomach by policemen and their nightsticks. I don't like to see young Negro kids—of seven, eight, nine-years-old—being thrown across the street by the force of a fire hose. But I believe that I must go down and say to the people down there, 'thank you for what you are doing ... not only for me and my children, but I believe for America.' So I'm going down to do whatever I possibly can.... Life is not a spectator sport. If you're going to spend your whole life in the grandstand just watching what goes on ...you're wasting your life."

—Jackie Robinson,
first African American to play Major League Baseball.

"I am so thankful I had the opportunity. I hope I set a good example and helped others who have come after me. It has been a wonderful life."

—Chuck Harmon, First Black Red.

Acknowledgements

Chuck and I thank you, the fans, for being interested in this all-American story. From the small town gyms and playing fields in Indiana, to the monolithic arenas and stadiums in America's great cities where world-class athletes like Chuck played, without the fans, baseball would be just a game.

We wrote this so the non-sports fan might like the story, too. If you want to find out how we got to where we are at now, you must look at where we have been. As I tell my kids, the world didn't start five years ago.

I thank Mr. Harmon and his wonderful family for allowing me to enter their lives over the past few years. A special recognition goes out to Bill and Tom Harmon and everyone at Harmon Construction, Inc. Without them, this project would not have been possible.

Of course, our families mean everything to us. They are our greatest accomplishment, and the source of our abiding love, passion, and pride. Both of us have many special people in our inner circles we love and cherish. We also thank the fine folks at the offices of the Cincinnati Reds and the Cincinnati Reds Hall of Fame. It seems as if we should personally thank about ten thousand people back in Chuck's wonderful hometown of Washington, Indiana

Dozens of books, articles, and people were used as resources for this book. We name many in the pages to follow, and there is a general guide at the end. We may have left out some folks, and we're sorry about that.

We hope to make the hours of taped interviews available on the Web. Chuck's story may be unique, but many fine writers, researchers, and fans gathered much of the surrounding information; in many cases we aggregated it in a new way. We apologize if we inadvertently left out the name of a person or a source. We tried very hard to verify and attribute properly and professionally, but some of these old stories are just that, something that somebody thinks they said or heard. Oral history sometimes blurs with the decades, but we have tried to find truth and fairness. The problem is, many times truth is found at the end of a long, lonely, path. In future editions we hope to clear up any shortcomings associated with our humble first attempt in telling you this story.

What we have created is a compilation of old and new information about the civil rights struggle in American sports, politics, and society. Along the way, we had a heck-of-a-lot of fun listening to and telling stories about some compelling characters. Bless them every one.

We thank God for our lives and our country. With all its bumps, bruises, and scars, America continues to be the most successful human experiment in world history.

For now, relax and mentally reach for your glove and bat, or just sit back in your imaginary bleachers and focus on a warm, clear, sunny day when hope and blue skies were all you could feel and all you could see and all you could ever hope for.

Once upon a time in America....

Marty Pieratt

To the love of my life, my Pearl, my wife, and my family
—*Chuck Harmon*

For all people of color who never had a fair chance, and for my mom.
She always believed in me, even when it didn't make much sense.
I guess that's why she said your mom is usually the
best friend you will have in life. She was right.
—*Marty Pieratt*

To Chelsey, Carter, Marlayna, Callie Jo...and little t

Contents

INTRODUCTION:
THE LIFE OF CHARLES BRYAN HARMON

EMORY ALLEN, CHUCK HARMON'S GREAT-GREAT GRANDFATHER, FOUGHT and died in the first all-Black regiment of the Civil War, made famous in the 1989 movie *Glory*. Allen died on November 30, 1864, on the battlefield at Honey Hill, South Carolina, fighting with the Massachusetts Colored Volunteer Infantry.

Stop and think: He died fighting for freedom in a country where he was not free himself. He died for his country, leaving behind seven children and his wife, Eliza. Sometimes courage seems to be a part of our DNA. Ninety years after his great-great-grandpa gave his life for America, Chuck walked out on a Cincinnati baseball field representing African Americans everywhere.

Telling the story of Charles Bryan "Chuck" Harmon has been a labor of love. To begin with, he is a wonderful human being. He has lived a grand life as a superb athlete, husband, father, brother, and friend. Chuck has been an excellent ambassador for Major League Baseball. With grace and grandeur, Chuck smiles and accepts all accolades and steps gently into his place in American history.

The way he handled himself after putting on the Cincinnati Reds uniform made a mockery of racism and helped bring about social change.

1

He wasn't what you call a great player in the major leagues. But when you consider his many accomplishments during a fifteen-season professional career, and the fact he was an African American pioneer surrounded by double standards and insults, Chuck Harmon's life is quite remarkable. Not only was he the first African American to suit up for the Reds, he nearly became the first Black in the National Basketball Association (NBA), playing for the Boston Celtics. He is thought to be the first Black coach in any professional sport. Throw in his high-school and college championships and titles—as well as a beautiful family and fascinating personal history—and this is one memorable guy, who most of us could stand to emulate. In this day of steroids and sex scandals, his story is pretty refreshing.

Beyond question, Chuck is an all-star gentleman who wanted to play ball and live life the right way. He has an incredible spirit of gratitude. "I have lived a great life," he says. "I got to meet Babe Ruth. I got to play with some of the best players ever, like Willie Mays, Hank Aaron, Joe DiMaggio, and Ted Williams. I have a great family and great friends. Why sure, it has been wonderful."

Cincinnati Reds broadcaster Thom Brennaman usually talks about stars of today, but he smiles when you mention Chuck Harmon. "He truly is a beloved figure around the ballpark," says Brennaman. "There are still people [alive] today who work at Great American Ballpark, who were at Crosley Field. They remember him and all the circumstances that were going on in the country around him when he came up with the Reds. I think people respect what he went through and the way he carries himself today. He is one of the kindest souls I have ever met."

According to Brennaman, Chuck is one of a handful of people who can walk into the WLW radio booth anytime they please. "In fact, you can count them on one hand.... Nobody has a fleeting or passing thought in their mind to stop him like they would anybody else. He comes up [to the radio booth at the stadium] and everything is A-OK. You know the people there are going want to see him."

If Chuck takes a notion to sit in back of the Reds radio broadcast box and say hello to Marty and Thom Brennaman, nobody says a word, other than "May I hold the elevator door for you, Mr. Harmon?"

Walt Jocketty, the Reds' president of baseball operations and general manager, echoes those feelings. "Chuck is special," he says. "He is a great, great person, and we love having him at the ballpark." "He attends all our events. I know it has been tough for him in the last few months [after the death of Chuck's wife], but he's is doing well, and we sure love having him around."

Chuck Harmon and veteran players like him are good for this tradition-rich franchise, says Rob Butcher, director of media relations for the Cincinnati Reds. "He really is one of the team and organization's ambassadors," says Butcher. "We do a lot of events out in the community and at the Reds Hall of Fame. Chuck is in the forefront of whatever we ask him to do. He represents us very well. We take care of him, and he takes care of us."

Butcher spends his days and nights taking care of today's games, players, publicity, and press needs. But he believes that what happened in the past is always relevant in baseball. "Even … players who don't know a whole lot historically [about what] happened in baseball know who Jackie Robinson is and what he did for the game. Most players coming into our organization don't know who Chuck Harmon is, but they eventually meet him and … and [realize] his significance to the organization. He's around a lot. We honor our history as well as any team in baseball, and Chuck is a very historic figure in Reds history. You can talk about Johnny Bench, and Pete Rose, and Joe Morgan; well, Chuck Harmon was a pioneer. He was the guy that opened it up for every African American player." Butcher continues, "Jackie Robinson had an edge to him; he would have had to have [one] with 20,000 screaming and wanting to hurt [him]. But Chuck is such a nice guy. I would have loved to have seen him on the field and his reaction and his demeanor and how he interacted with the fans at that time. He and Joe Nuxhall [the late Reds pitcher and broadcaster] were maybe the nicest guys you would ever meet in your life. Neither had a bad word to say about anybody."

In fact, Nuxhall, who was in the dugout when Harmon made his first appearance, may have said it best. About ten years ago, he told the *Cincinnati Enquirer*, "Charley was such a first-class person that he fit in right away."

Chuck's personality is a result of his family and community, and a personal, passionate commitment to be above the fray. His life story begins with a sweet, little kid minding his parents and adoring his eleven siblings —all of whom were squeezed into a little two-story house in bucolic Washington, Indiana. He loved to go to the local basketball courts and baseball fields where he honed skills that would put him among the elite athletes of the world. He went on to play in most of the major cities in the United States and quite a few outside the country. More than a million people saw Chuck play baseball and basketball. If you could talk to them, I would dare you to find a one who doubted Chuck Harmon's skill on the field or his character once the game was done.

Today, you can still find him looking forward to his next trip to the old ball field. The eyes that once pounced on ninety-five-mile-per-hour fastballs now find it difficult to drive, but he's always up for some baseball. He attends many Reds games, passing out his autographed card to little kids with big, bright eyes. One card shows a young, strong Harmon with piercing eyes, baseball in hand, ready to whip it back to another player. In another, his bat is cocked and ready to explode on a baseball. He wears the uniform of the day proudly, Cincinnati written across his cotton jersey and a "C" on his cap. The bottom of the card says "The Power of Tradition." That's pretty much the way Chuck would like to be remembered. He is thankful he played for the Philadelphia Phillies and St. Louis Cardinals—and that he was one of the first African Americans to play for those teams—but his heart is with the Cincinnati Reds.

Rick Walls, executive director of the Reds Hall of Fame and Museum, calls Chuck an icon. "We are very fortunate to have somebody like Chuck Harmon. He is always present at events and never hesitates to support the museum," Walls says, referencing the spectacular 15,000-square-foot building adjacent to Great American Ballpark. It may be the best baseball museum in the world other than the National Baseball Hall of Fame in Cooperstown, New York. "Chuck is not in the [national] Hall of Fame, but he's a hall of famer in the eyes of many. He persevered through difficult times. His story has significance for all of us."

How wonderful it is that Chuck has been honored by the Reds Hall of Fame and Museum next to the stadium. Just a few base hits down the street is another museum, the National Underground Railroad Freedom Center, which opened in 2004. In less than a decade, nearly a million people from all fifty states and dozens of countries have visited this symbolic museum, which tells the story of the brave men and women who helped destroy slavery by creating a secret network of escape routes. All this was situated along the Ohio River, which at one time separated the slave from the free. As you will find out later, Chuck's story, maybe his life, begins with people along the Ohio River who believed passionately in freedom for all. One of the historic escape routes was not far from his Indiana home.

But when Chuck goes to the games these days, he doesn't ponder as much about social change as he does about the pitching or hitting strength of the Reds. He still can play all the games in his mind. He watches batters and says aloud what the player at the plate should be thinking. "It's a three and two count. He can't watch the ball go by. He's got to make contact, if it's close.... You know, they should take more infield practice ... they should work more on bunting." You can tell that he lives for those visits to the ballpark.

However, though his mind is ready to play a doubleheader, his body is in its last innings. He walks slowly to his box seats along the first baseline; sometimes, he even takes a wheelchair part of the way. On days when he is feeling good, he walks with the swagger and confidence of a much younger man. In his eyes, you can see the satisfaction of a life well lived and well loved. At Great American Baseball Park is a plaque honoring his accomplishment as the first African American to play for the Reds. It's on the outside wall, near the main gate.

Chuck may have been to the athletic mountaintop before he ever stepped to the plate wearing the Cincinnati Reds uniform. He and his Washington High School Hatchets won back-to-back Indiana state high-school basketball championships in 1941 and 1942. Not only was this before Jackie Robinson broke the color barrier in baseball, it was before African Americans were allowed to play basketball in the Big Ten; that would happen seven years later just up the road from Chuck's hometown on the campus of Indiana University (IU). Bill Garrett of Shelbyville, Indiana, was the first Black to cross that line.

Many of the crowds who watched Chuck play during his Indiana school days were larger than those at major league stadiums. It's estimated that he played before nearly 200,000 fans during his high-school career. His high-

5

school gym had 4,323 seats even though the town had only about 9,000 people. Today there are even fewer people, but the new gym seats just over 7,000. The school has six state basketball titles under its belt and is looking forward to more. It's a college basketball player factory. Chuck is proud to be part of that tradition, too.

In Chuck's day, the state championships were held at Hinkle Fieldhouse in Indianapolis, made famous lately by the hoop dreams of the Cinderella team at Butler University. It also is where the final scenes of *Hoosiers* were filmed. It was packed with 14,000 spectators each year Chuck led his team to the title, competing against about 700 other teams in a one-and-out, single-class state tournament.

But although in Indiana Chuck may be known best for his young basketball days, his place in civil rights history is because he was the first Black Red.

I first met Chuck while I was a reporter for WLWT Channel 5, the NBC affiliate in Cincinnati. It was the 1990 World Series. As the Reds were sweeping the Oakland Athletics, a controversy was simmering between then Reds star Eric Davis (now special assistant to the general manager) and Reds owner Marge Schott. After he injured himself crashing into a wall, Davis said that Mrs. Schott didn't see to his medical needs as she should have and he had to rent a jet and pay for his trip back to Cincinnati to see doctors. It led to a discussion about whether Black players were treated differently in any way, though Mrs. Schott told me in television interviews and off the camera that she was offended people would think that.

I remembered that a friend of mine from high school, Bill Harmon, had an uncle who was one of the earliest Black players for the Reds. I wondered what he thought of the hot topic of the day. Bill, who was an outstanding basketball player at the University of Louisville, helped me track down his Uncle Chuck at the Hamilton County courthouse, where he worked for many years as the deputy clerk and administrative assistant for the Ohio First District Court of Appeals.

Chuck agreed to the interview, and he was his usual warm and friendly self—the man he always was, the man he always will be. During our interview, he had no harsh words for either Mr. Davis or Mrs. Schott, but he smiled and clearly indicated that the situation for Black players had come a long way since he stepped on Crosley Field amid murmurs in the stands and strange looks and cold shoulders from teammates. In Chuck's day, Black players weren't always welcome at the same restaurants and hotels as the White players. He didn't say anything too direct about what the difference might be for a modern Black player, but you could understand what he was thinking when he said, "Oh, yes, it is very different today." Chuck simply was glad to have helped pave the way, as did his friends Jackie Robinson, Hank Aaron, Willie Mays, and Larry Doby.

By my recollection, it was after that television story that Chuck became certified as the first Black Red. He became a frequent source for local TV, radio, and newspaper reporters when they needed perspective from the first African American Cincinnati Red, who stepped out onto the field and walked into the history books. He is still a media favorite today.

Chuck's first appearance at Crosley Field came on April 17, 1954. It was about a month after tiny Milan made history by winning the Indiana High School Basketball Championship, the basis for *Hoosiers*, what Sports Illustrated called the best sports movie ever. It was just four days after Hank Aaron made his debut as the first Black player on the Milwaukee Braves, when Milwaukee beat the Braves on opening day in Cincinnati, 9 to 8. President Dwight Eisenhower was telling Americans not to get so worked up about atomic bombs, and Senator Joe McCarthy was telling anybody who would listen that Communists had us surrounded.

Reds owner Powell Crosley, General Manager Gabe Paul, and Manager Birdie Tebbetts made the decision that it was time for Cincinnati to break the color line. They waited until the Reds were on the road. A few games into the season on a bright, cool spring afternoon against the Braves at Milwaukee County stadium, Charles Harmon stepped to the plate wearing a Cincinnati Reds uniform. His number was "10." The young, Black infielder popped out. The Reds lost 5 to 1. History had been made in Cincinnati. The color line had been erased, and the franchise has never looked back.

Just a couple innings before Harmon batted, Nino Escalera, a Puerto Rican player of African descent, batted and hit a single. It would be his only season in the Big Leagues, but he is remembered as the eighth Puerto Rican to play in the majors, and the first lefthander to play shortstop. According to Reds historian Greg Rhodes, the Reds were the ninth big league team to ᴀck players. The Boston Red Sox were the last, doing so in July 's appearance came seven years after Jackie Robinson broke ᴜarrier.

First there was Chuck for the Reds, and then soon after came his teammate, the great Frank Robinson, the first MVP player in both leagues and the first African American to manage a major league team, again in both leagues. Then came all the great Black players like Joe Black, Vada Pinson, Bobby Tolan, Lee May, Joe Morgan, George Foster, and Barry Larkin. The list could go on and on. Today, Reds fans can't imagine them not being a part of the proud tradition of the Reds, baseball's first professional team. But Chuck was the first. He paved the way.

Chuck had about a four-year career, spending it with the Reds, Cardinals, and Phillies, but Cincinnati became his home. He worked for years helping sell sporting equipment to big names like Willie Mays, Hank Aaron, and his buddy Pete Rose for McGregor Sporting Goods, and was a scout in Latin America, mostly for the San Francisco Giants and New York Mets. He did some NBA scouting for the Indiana Pacers, too.

By telling Chuck's story, I am able to drift just a few degrees closer to my childhood heroes, like Cincinnati's Pete Rose and Johnny Bench, guys Chuck knows on a first-name basis and whom I have been able to meet because of my work in journalism. Pete isn't allowed to attend official functions because of his suspension, but he has been known to sit down by Chuck in the stands and talk baseball. The Reds kindly give their senior ambassador season tickets.

This book project was made even more fun because of roots Chuck and I share. We both love sports and are from Southern Indiana. I'd loved the Reds since I was an eleven-year-old paper boy for the *Cincinnati Post* in a village about seventy miles west of Cincinnati in Butlerville, Indiana, and then when I was on the air for the NBC television station in the Queen City. I had to try to keep my composure around Bench and Rose, who were often seen walking around our office and studio. To me, they were icons. If you are an old Big Red Machine fan like I am, they still are.

Now that I teach at IU back in Bloomington, I still root for the Reds and no other team. I still love to come back to the ballpark to see the new guys and remember days gone by. Of course, I'm proud to hang with Chuck, a guy who was a respected friend of so many legends, and maybe just as cool. He treats the guys that sell peanuts the same way he does those who are in the Hall of Fame.

I can close my eyes and smell cigars and stale beer at old Crosley Field and hear the crack of the bat, the slap of the ball in the glove, that steady roar of the crowd. That's where I saw my first Reds game, thanks to my little league coach Bob Bishop. I can still feel the thunder of the Big Red Machine when I attended the first doubleheader at Riverhead Stadium in Cincinnati, and I remember the day my dad banged on Rose's window and demanded he give me an autograph. Pete did so without hesitation. Years later, I would be one of the first to go on the air outside the U.S. Federal Courthouse in downtown Cincinnati with the news that Pete Rose, the Cincinnati Reds player-manager and the greatest hitter of all-time, would go to prison for income tax evasion. My colleague, Steve Forest, was covering the story, but the judge wouldn't dismiss the courtroom until Pete was on his way. My station called me off a story in northern Kentucky, and I believe I was the first to break the news. We cut into a soap opera for what became heart-wrenching reality TV for Reds fans.

Pete refused to talk to us when we visited his prison home in Marion, Ohio. But later, when he quietly left prison, his attorney Reuben Katz, let us know when he would show up in Cincinnati. We had the exclusive story as Pete helped cook lunch for poor kids in a troubled neighborhood. He gave me a funny look while we were putting the story together, grinned, and said, "Why don't you help out, Marty, and hand me that big can of fruit cocktail?" I did. I felt like I had to hustle for Mr. Hustle.

A few days later we followed Pete as he walked into Riverfront Stadium for the first time after the scandal the rocked baseball and devastated Cincinnati. It marked the first time he had to sit in the ballpark like a regular fan. I remember looking at his face and thinking about how much he loved baseball. He'd said, "I'd walk through hell in a gasoline suit to play baseball." If you were lucky enough to see Pete play, you know he was telling the truth. I see the number 14 today, and I can't help but think of Pete.

Today, Chuck considers Pete a good friend. Chuck doesn't get riled up about anything, unless it's whether Pete Rose should be in the Hall of Fame.

He thinks it's a joke the guy with the most hits isn't there. Chuck and other Black players have not forgotten that Pete treated them equally back when baseball integration was a fresh and tender issue. If you were a restaurant, hotel, or ballplayer who didn't treat all players alike, I'm told that Pete might have pretended you were Ray Fosse blocking the plate.

Fosse was the Cleveland catcher physically plastered on the last play of the 1970 All-Star game. He stood between a hard-charging Rose and the winning run. Pete was the bull. Fosse became the China shop. Some say Fosse is still seeing stars. Rose was criticized for injuring Fosse and playing so fiercely in an exhibition game.

That makes Chuck laugh.

That tickles Pete.

Rose was there to win.

He got it done.

That's the way most everybody played in the 1950s. That's when Pete was a kid just watching at Crosley Field. Pete's beloved dad Harry was famous for his athletic intensity, and Pete was an excellent student of the smash-nose baseball he watched, maybe that's one of the reasons he would get frustrated at some injury-prone modern players when he managed - if Pete had a bone exposed, he would still try to play a few innings.

That's the kind of guy he was. Mr. Harmon was pretty close.

When I talked with Pete about Chuck's life story, he was more than glad to reminisce from his home in Las Vegas.

"Chuck knows I never did care what color your skin was. Chuck understood how hard I worked," said baseball's all-time hit king. "That's probably why he always liked me. It was my style of play. Chuck was a good player. A hustler. Good speed. He played hard. He had the same style as me. I just had a better opportunity," Rose said.

Rose remembers going to the ballpark with his dad as a youngster with big dreams, especially when the Dodgers and hometown hero Don Zimmer were in town. Chuck remembers the two hanging around outside the clubhouse. The 1950s style of play was tough and tenacious. Rose learned that style watching as a kid, and knew no other way to go about baseball and life. "Those guys in the 50's, it was play as hard as you can and take no prisoners."

The young Rose would grow up and ruffle feathers about nine years later in 1963 when the Reds decided the hometown rookie should start at second base on a World Series caliber team. Resentment among some White veterans made Rose an isolated part of the team, until a couple of African Americans reached out a hand to the vivacious new kid with a crew cut and merciless determination.

"I was called into the Reds office for hanging with the Black guys," Rose remembered in late April of 2010. "I told them Frank Robinson and Vada Pinson treated me with respect. Those guys understood how hard I worked. They gave me a chance. I'm not saying they were racist or anything, but the Reds management was concerned about me being with the Black players, but those were the guys who actually treated me like one of the players on the team. They were very nice to me and always treated me with respect."

Time has healed almost all wounds. Rose earned the respect of his teammates and management that year and was named the league's rookie of the year. He became one of the best to ever play. If you were on his team, you usually loved it. If you were his opponent, keep your head low. He would remove it to win, playing just like Chuck and those guys in the 1950s.

Like Chuck, Rose tries to look on the bright side these days. He is proud Chuck steadfastly believes Rose should be in the Hall of Fame.

"I've been a friend of Chuck's for many years. He played hard like me. He was always good for the team because he had such a great personality. He helped everybody to become better. That's why people like him. He is so positive. Chuck's a good man."

Without hesitation, Chuck says the same thing about Pete Rose.

If it were up to him, Pete would be in the Hall right now.

A few of my Cincinnati stories will make their way into this fantastic story of Chuck Harmon. He transcends more than sixty years of Reds baseball and civil rights history. He was there way before players like Rose and Bench. He also paved the way for players like Ken Griffey, both senior and junior; the younger Griffey is as close as anybody to Chuck outside his family, even though he plays in Seattle. Chuck hangs around the ballpark today, cheering on the Reds and hoping for a resurgence of the national pastime among American youth, especially Black kids. It's hard for Chuck to believe that less than 10 percent of big league ballplayers are African American.

He thinks it is still a beautiful game, played in special, park-like places by brilliant athletes at a pace that is refreshing. There is no clock to watch. There is no rush to finish. Everybody is just trying to find home.

No matter how nice Chuck is, and no matter how he refuses to say hardly a smattering of a negative word about anybody or anything, this man was a pioneer and a trailblazer. Without men of character and decency like Jackie Robinson and Charles Harmon—who excelled and kept their composure when most of us could not or would not—we would not have a President Barack Obama. We might not have gained so much ground so quickly in America. Just eighty-nine years before Chuck played along the Mason-Dixon Line in Cincinnati, slavery was legal. Long after that bigotry was tolerated and still is, in some parts.

Chuck is a solid brick in the foundation of American civil rights and the efforts to achieve a truly free and equal America. His story may be small compared to that of Dr. Martin Luther King, Jr., and others who fought for the passage of the Civil Rights Act, but it is a story that reminds us that good things still happen to good people who strive to do well, tell the truth, and are honest and decent. Chuck's story makes us feel better about an America that seems to be rocked by violence and scandal and disappointments of heroic proportions. As former New York Yankee Tommy John told me, "It's important that we remember the way it was." John, like Chuck, is in the Indiana Baseball Hall of Fame.

Oscar Robertson was one of the best basketball players ever. After winning two championships with Crispus Attucks High School in Indianapolis, he dominated at the University of Cincinnati and became a hall of famer in the NBA. He is the only player in NBA history to average a triple-double for an entire season. He is on everyone's all-time NBA team. He battled prejudice all along the way. He thinks Chuck's place in history is very important to remember.

"I think it's great. When he came along there weren't many Blacks in baseball. He was such a gentleman and a good baseball player that he raised the bar for Black players."

The "Big O" led his all-Black high-school basketball team to a 62 to 1 record during Chuck's first two years with the Reds. Robertson hasn't forgotten that the Indianapolis police told his fans they could only celebrate at a designated African American park, not downtown driving Cadillacs backward around the Circle as Milan had done the previous year.

"We won," says Robertson. "We were from Indianapolis. We were the first undefeated team. But didn't get celebrate downtown like Milan and all the other teams that won. I understand what they were doing it.... It was a White-Black thing.... I'm not going to forgive them, but I'm beyond it. When stuff happens to you when you are seventeen years old, why should you forget it?"

He and athletes like Jackie Robinson may have been more outspoken than Chuck, but he says Harmon changed society in his own quiet way. "You want to make sure you succeed," says Robertson. "That's what you do first. Then you address the issues. I'm sure he did what he had to do. He's a great, great ambassador for baseball."

Chuck should be proud. The Harmon family should be proud. Cincinnati should be proud, and so should America. The work for equal rights is far from done, but it's nice to look back and see our accomplishments. If you let it all sink in a little, it is clear we have come a long, long way, and it gives you great hope for what lies ahead. Hopefully, as Abraham Lincoln said, we can all be touched "by the better angels of our nature."

THAT SPECIAL SPRING

PHIL COX REMEMBERS THAT WONDERFUL SPRING IN Cincinnati when it happened. The baseball team he loved and adored would have an African American on the roster. The truly first Black Red.

He was just seven years old. He lived at 830 Oliver Street in Cincinnati's West End, just four blocks from an unbelievable structure. Crosley Field. Home of the Reds. It said so in huge letters on the grandstand wall facing outside the mammoth concrete and steel structure.

Phil went to school just one block from Crosley at Sands Elementary. His mostly Black school was at the corner of Findlay Street and Freeman Avenue. The Reds, baseball's oldest professional team, established in 1869, had played at Findlay Street and Western Avenue in various grandstands and under various names since 1884. The park was so close if Phil fell asleep, his dad would carry him home, then return to watch the end of the ball game. Fans could sit in the sun deck for seventy-five cents. The best seats were just a couple of bucks.

Of course, being just outside the park was pretty cool, too, especially for the kids. Sometimes it was worth skipping school to try to catch home-run balls that came over the left-field fence in the alley between the wall and the large laundry building. Drive north on Interstate 75, look to the left not far from Union Terminal and that's where it was—and still is, in thousands of imaginations.

Even being at home was almost like being there. Phil could hear the roar of the crowds from his bedroom. That's pretty heavy stuff for a little boy who loved baseball. "I would play baseball all day until I couldn't play anymore," he says.

Crosley Field was the monolithic stadium where superstars played the mighty American game of baseball. Of course, there were just White stars at that time and almost no Black players. But even though the Reds didn't have any Black players, they didn't have much of a problem getting Black fans to spend their money to get into the ballpark. A few African American players from other teams had come to Cincinnati, such as the Brooklyn Dodger's Jackie Robinson, the Giants' Willie Mays, and the Milwaukee Brave's Hank Aaron, the last just four days before opening day in 1954. Although there were no African Americans on their hometown team, for Phil and his buddies it felt weird to cheer against Cincinnati.

"Those ballplayers were like gods to kids, but they had to stay in homes and hotels that would accept Blacks," Cox says. "When Jackie and the Dodgers would come to town, Black people would come out in droves. I really didn't understand it then. I kind of thought they were traitors. The Reds were our team."

But on April 17, 1954, any confusion about allegiance to the home team stopped like a runner sliding into home plate. This day would be like no other because the Cincinnati Reds announced there would a Black player in the lineup alongside legends like Joe Nuxhall, Ted Kluszewski, Gus Bell, Johnny Temple, and Wally Post. The new player's number would be "10." His name? Chuck Harmon. He was a young man from Indiana who had made headlines as a basketball player and a terrific hitter in baseball's minor leagues.

Among the folks in Phil's neighborhood, the excitement was palatable. "We were all amazed and proud. I remember how they would say it back then, 'now the Reds have a colored player,'" Cox says. "It made you think this is something special. People would talk about Chuck Harmon and how fast he was."

Being able to hear the crowds and see the lights certainly helped make young Phil become a baseball fan. But seeing tall, handsome, athletic, smiling Chuck Harmon wearing the Reds uniform sent him to an all-new level. He collected baseball cards like most kids, but now he had the opportunity to have a Reds card with the image of a ballplayer who looked like him. "It was a very special thing," Cox says. "It was the happiest time of my life. It was almost euphoric. We were poor, but we weren't really because we were loved. Our folks taught us that we were not better than anybody else, but we were certainly as good as anybody else."

Phil's family could not eat in all the restaurants in Cincinnati or use some of the public restrooms or pools. But Chuck Harmon's arrival was maybe, just maybe, a sign that things were going to change.

"Chuck's appearance into baseball moved all of us in the community," Cox says more than fifty-five years later. "It was an inspiration to all of us. He was a genuine hero to us. To see somebody get to that level, knowing how difficult it was at that time, it was fantastic."

To truly understand how dramatic Chuck Harmon's appearance was, one has to imagine what life was like in Cincinnati back then. It was the southernmost team in the big leagues, and the ballpark was located smack dab in the city's most densely populated African American neighborhood. What Blacks called home, Whites called "slums."

"If I had this to do this all over again, I do wish we would have appreciated Chuck Harmon more when he first came to the Reds," says Cox. "It was so rare to see Black people succeed like that. Back then, if a Black entertainer or person was on TV, you would call your friends and relatives and gather around and watch. It was so seldom you saw it."

In the 1950s, Cox's neighborhood, once the home of immigrant Germans, was home to thousands of African Americans who had moved from the rural South to the urban North in the preceding decades. For many, Cincinnati was the first stop in an attempt for a more free and better life. After two centuries of slavery, Black Americans were trying to find a special place to call home.

The era between the world wars witnessed the biggest resettlement of our country's population. It was a demographic earthquake. In many ways, Cincinnati was right in the middle of this human shift. Beginning in the 1940s and especially after the war, Black families took a liking to Cincinnati. It was more north than south and more east than west. With a population of just under a half-million, the city was a great place for anybody to find a job. There were lots of positions in factories and businesses tied to such powerhouse firms as Proctor & Gamble and General Electric. The post-World War II world needed plenty of soap and jet engines, and Cincinnati workers—Black and White—were more than willing to oblige.

In 1950, the U.S. Census estimated that Cincinnati's Black population was about 80,000 people, three-quarters of whom lived in the West End near the baseball park. If not for the friendly feel of the concrete and steel stadium, White Cincinnatians may never have seen the West End. The neighborhood around Crosley Field was not a chamber of commerce photo opportunity. There was a lot of tenement housing, old factories, railroad tracks, and empty lots. There was hardly any parking, one of the reasons the city wanted the Reds to move to the riverfront downtown in 1970. The neighborhoods were teeming with residents. Many Black people who moved north to the Queen City would squeeze into small places until they could afford something bigger and better.

By the time Chuck showed up in a pressed Reds uniform with a big "C" on his chest, city planners already were thinking about building interstates through the West End and tearing down Crosley Field and the hundreds of homes that surrounded it. With no elected representative, those who lived in the West End would have little to say about it.

By today's standards, the West End wasn't much of a neighborhood. But make no mistake about it, on that beautiful spring day in 1954, there was intense community pride. From that point on, every game would be like a holiday. Black Cincinnatians no longer had to wait until Jackie Robinson or Willie Mays came to town to be a part of the American pastime. Chuck Harmon was now a Cincinnati Red, a team that was aggressive, explosive, and had a good chance of going all the way. He reminded a lot of Reds fans of Jackie Robinson, the Brooklyn Dodger star. Chuck was tall, athletic, and quick. He walked with self-confidence. He was a college man with an air of sophistication.

Just as young Black kids like Phil were watching the civil rights struggle in baseball, so were the White kids. One of them was another young Reds fan, who lived in a very different neighborhood, west of the West End. Paul "Ham" Wernke was a baseball prospect at the time. He lived in Batesville, Indiana, about fifty miles west of Crosley Field. He has been a Reds fan all his life. "If you lived in Batesville, you had to be a Reds fan," Wernke says. "My dad would sit and the backyard and listen on the radio everyday."

Wernke got the chance to go see the Reds at Crosley in the 1940s, on Knothole Day at the ballpark when he could get in free. Every now and then, his dad would make the big trip. But not too often. "A 1932 Plymouth or a 1949 Chevy wasn't made to drive to Cincinnati every day," Wernke says.

Seeing Black players on the opposing team was unusual for Wernke and his teammates. "There were no Blacks in Batesville at the time," he says. In 1952, Wernke's Bulldog basketball team was rolling to the Sweet Sixteen of Indiana's state high-school tournament. That is, until they ran into Indianapolis's Crispus Attucks High School and Oscar Robertson's big brother, Bailey. It was then that Wernke first competed against African Americans and saw firsthand their ability and determination. Three years later, Oscar and his Attucks teammates would be the first all-Black team to win a state championship. Over two seasons, Attucks went a combined 45–1, winning consecutive state tournaments with 752 teams in 1955 and 742 teams in 1956.

When Chuck Harmon was called up in 1954, Wernke was slugging and pitching for the Florida State Seminoles. He'd left the cold winters near Cincinnati to play baseball and basketball in Tallahassee. His coach was a former Reds player, Danny Litwhiler (1948–51). The news about a Black Reds player made its way to the Sunshine State. Jackie Robinson was a household name, so it only made sense for the Reds to be as good as they could be and sign a quality player like Chuck.

"Absolutely," says Wernke. "You could just see how hard he played and so determined. That's why Black ballplayers succeeded." Wernke always had thought it was odd that Black players weren't in the majors. "We knew there were Negro Leagues and great players like Satchel Paige, but we never got to see just how great they were." Wernke spent his college summers playing in the now-defunct Tri-County League. Most of its teams were just west of Cincinnati in southeast Indiana towns such as Batesville, Oldenburg, and Sunman. It would later boast two major leaguers, Dyar Miller (New York Mets, Baltimore Orioles, California Angels, Toronto Blue Jays) and Jim Lyttle (New York Yankees, Los Angles Dodgers, Chicago White Sox, Montreal Expos). Even that league allowed Black players. "Mr. Boston would bring the team in from the city in an old bus. He later had a son who played in the big leagues," says Wernke, referring to Daryl Boston, who played for the Mets, White Sox, Rockies, and Yankees between 1984 and 1994. Daryl Boston was part of Colorado's inaugural team and hit the fiftieth home run off Bert Blyleven in 1985, the record for the most homers allowed in one season.

One summer, a couple of college basketball buddies from the University of Cincinnati (UC), Jack Twyman and Ace Moorman, mentioned that there was a kid who might want to play for Wernke's team to stay in shape for the summer, but he was really a basketball player. They told Wernke this Jewish kid from Brooklyn had such a hot arm that only one guy at UC, Danny Gilbert, would catch him. "We were told he threw really hard and might help us out. But if he [hit] somebody … he would kill them."

The kid's name was Sandy Koufax.

Koufax eventually got the control thing down. He was drafted by the Dodgers and became a three-time Cy Young award winner who tossed four no-hitters. He threw a perfect game on September 9, 1965; not one of the twenty-seven batters he faced reached first base. He became the youngest player inducted to the National Baseball Hall of Fame and today works for the Dodgers' front office.

Wernke and many others find it interesting that Koufax played with Jackie Robinson and the Dodgers. Jewish Americans and African Americans can identify with each other as persecuted minorities. The two groups seem to always be near the top of the hate list of the Ku Klux Klan. Koufax stirred controversy by playing in a 1965 World Series game that fell on the Jewish sacred day of Yom Kippur. Robinson reportedly thought early on that Koufax should pitch more and clashed with Dodger manager Walter Alston over it. Koufax eventually got all the work he wanted. He earned his first win against the Reds on August 27, 1955, in a 7–0, complete-game shutout. On September 29, 1957, he became the last man to pitch for the

Dodgers before the team moved to Los Angeles and broke a million hearts in Brooklyn.

Ironically, Wernke might have played in the major leagues if Jackie Robinson had not opened the door to baseball integration. In 1956, he tried out for the Reds but went home with no offers. By then, most of the big league teams and nearly all minor league teams were signing talented Black players. "I don't know if I would have made it, but it made a difference," says Wernke. "But [allowing Blacks to play] was the right thing to do.... There were a lot of guys playing before the Blacks came in [who] obviously would not have been playing had [Blacks] been there."

Today, Ham Wernke is a retired high-school athletic director. He still loves baseball. So does Phil Cox.

Phil Cox is sixty-two and an accomplished Cincinnati businessman. Now chairman of the board of Cincinnati Bell, he was the first and only African American chief executive officer of a major corporation in Cincinnati. He serves on the boards of several other global companies and was president of the board of trustees for the University of Cincinnati. Cox says that Chuck Harmon and others like him set the tone for his life.

"What he did and the course that he set was an immense inspiration to me, along with my parents. They taught us to grow and get better. He was a big part of that. We're all just a link in the chain, we are not the chain. We have to honor those who preceded us and inspired us.

"I hope I have honored him and have provided an inspiration for those who will follow me. His impact went far beyond sports and baseball. It's inspiration that touches the hearts of a lot of people. The most important thing about leadership is an example, and he was a good example. He came along at a time that is hard for any of us to understand or relate."

Phil Cox and his family certainly took the lesson to heart. He was the first Black to graduate from Saint Xavier High School. His brother, Lamar, is thought to be the first Black to graduate from the University of Cincinnati's engineering school. "The professor would ask if anybody objected to sitting next to him. If they did, he would try to find a[nother] seat. You imagine what it did to the psyche."

The son of a Georgia sharecropper and a maid, and a great-grandson of a slave, Cox says that Chuck Harmon's life is not just a great story about Black achievement but a great American story that can inspire us all.

"Look how far we have come. It's because of the courage and character of people like Chuck Harmon that we have the kind of country we do have today. Imagine what it took to do it. All of us have to admire men and women like that, and those who made the choice to accept and support them."

But why Chuck Harmon? Why was he the first Black Red in Cincinnati? Well, that's another story.

Why Chuck Harmon?

To answer the question, "why Chuck?" we first should try to figure out why it took seven years after the Dodgers broke the barrier for the Reds to follow suit. Before that, why did the powers that be in baseball refuse to allow African Americans to play? The answer is complicated, but it begins with tradition, ignorance, and bigotry.

Like everything, you must take it in the context of the time. Rather than being judgmental, maybe we should thank those brave people who stood up to make a difference. In the end, the Cincinnati Reds organization became a leader in our country's civil rights movement even if those running the club didn't know it at the time.

Baseball was played in America before the Civil War started in 1861. The Civil War may have given Blacks freedom in theory, but not in practice. That was certainly true in baseball. As early as 1867, there were reports of prejudice on the playing field. The *Philadelphia Inquirer* reported the all-Black Philadelphia Pythians were banned from what was then the National Association of Base Ball Players, which declared itself "against the admission of any clubs composed of colored men...." In 1883, Cap Anson, star of the Chicago White Stockings, refused to play against the Toledo Blue Stockings unless African American catcher Moses "Fleetwood" Walker left the field. Only when he was told he would have to forfeit receipts from the fans did he agree to play.

Walker was born in Mount Pleasant, Ohio, the son of one of the first African American physicians in Ohio, Dr. Moses W. Walker. He played on Oberlin College's first baseball team in 1881. He went to the University of Michigan Law School the next year and played for one of the Wolverines first baseball teams. In those days, teams like Toledo and the Louisville Eclipse were considered part of the major leagues. Thus, Walker and his brother, Welday, are considered the first African Americans to play in the big leagues. But before their careers could really get started, all leagues banned Black players and refused to sign contracts with them even in the minors.

As a result, barnstorming teams of Black players began to travel the country to show their skills, and many Negro Leagues were formed. For decades, the leagues drew huge attendance and interest. Whether the teams were playing in the big-city stadiums while the White teams were out of town or in their own parks, or were barnstorming across the nation, Negro League baseball gave superb players an opportunity and became one of the first highly successful Black-owned industries in the United States. Cincinnati's Crosley Field is believed to be the first park to rent its space to a Black team, the Cuban Stars.

In 1920, Andrew "Rube" Foster created the seven-team Negro National League. That same year the six-team Negro Southern League debuted. Three years later, six teams would comprise the Eastern Colored League. In 1937, seven teams were organized, and the Negro American League was born, including the Kansas City Monarchs, a team that later would feature Leroy "Satchel" Paige, a player Chuck Harmon eventually got to play with and against in exhibition games. The Homestead Grays would feature Josh Gibson, called the "Black Babe Ruth." Chuck Harmon played five games for the Indianapolis Clowns under a fake name, Charley Fine, because he wanted to keep his eligibility to play basketball and baseball at the University of Toledo.

Cincinnati certainly had a decent amount of influence in the leagues. The Cincinnati Tigers were put together by DeHart Hubbard, the first African American to win a gold medal. In the early 1940s, the Cincinnati Buckeyes competed in the Negro Leagues. Cincinnati and Indianapolis shared a franchise known as the Clowns, which was the Negro League team on which Chuck played. The great Satchel Paige played for the Cincinnati Crescents in the fall of 1946. Charlie Davis, a close friend of Harmon's who currently lives in Cincinnati, played for the Memphis Red Sox.

Things finally started changing when the Brooklyn Dodgers signed Jackie Robinson to the minor leagues in 1945. After playing with Montreal in the international league, he broke the color barrier in the major leagues on April 15, 1947. What once seemed impossible for Harmon, now was possible.

"I didn't think because Jackie made it, I was going to make it," Harmon says. "I just thought, well, they're signing Black players, and if I'm good enough, I'll be there."

Larry Doby, a friend and navy teammate of Harmon's, was signed the next year by the Cleveland Indians and became the first Black in the American League. Also in 1948, the old legend, Satchel Paige, became the oldest rookie ever after he signed to play for the Indians. He became the first Black to pitch in a World Series. By 1952, 150 Negro League players had been integrated into the major leagues, so those old leagues went out of existence. But racism did not.

There is a hint of racism today, depending on whom you talk to or which studies you ponder. But during the 1940s and 1950s, there was an epidemic of hate and intolerance, even around Cincinnati. The Reds were the southernmost team, and although prejudice is found everywhere, during that time it was noticeably more of a problem in the South. The old Confederacy was still stinging from the Civil War loss in 1865 and the subsequent federal troop occupation for more than a decade. Some have said it was worse for Black people in the South in 1965 than it was in 1865. In the years before the turn of the twentieth century, "peacekeeping " soldiers headed North and the country had other cares than demanding democracy for former slaves in places like Alabama, Georgia, or Mississippi.

There was never an official rule against Blacks playing in the major leagues. It was a gentlemen's agreement between the owners. Commissioner, Kennesaw "Mountain" Landis, born near Cincinnati in Millville and raised in Logansport, Indiana, was vehemently opposed to integration and joined with the owners to fight it at all levels of professional baseball. However, once Kentucky's Albert "Happy" Chandler took over for Landis, things changed. Happy was ready to break down the walls, and he found in Branch Rickey of the Dodgers an owner who was ready to start smashing those walls with a super sledgehammer, even though every other owner at the time was against it.

Ohio should be proud of Rickey. He fought unanimous opposition and won. He was born in Little California near Portsmouth on December 20, 1881. He grew up loving the Cincinnati Reds. He became a catcher for the Ohio Wesleyan University team, which had a Black player by the name of Charles Thomas from Zanesville, Ohio. Thomas was used to playing ball with Whites. He and Louis F. Colston were on the 1901 Zanesville High School football team. But he found life difficult at the college level.

Branch Rickey never forgot how Thomas was treated when the team faced the University of Kentucky, whose varsity refused to play, and Notre Dame a few weeks later. The clerk at a South Bend, Indiana, hotel refused to allow Thomas to stay there until Rickey said he would take the whole team elsewhere. Only then was Thomas allowed to stay in Rickey's room. Once in the room, Thomas began to sob convulsively and rub hard at the skin on his arms as if he were trying to remove his color. According to a September 1947 article by Mark Harris in *Negro Digest*, Rickey told the catcher, "Someday, somehow, we will do something about the whole business of discrimination." Rickey was later quoted as saying, "Whatever mark that incident left on the Black boy, it was no more indelible than the impressions made on me."

Thomas, later a New Mexico dentist, said in that 1947 article that by signing Jackie Robinson to the Dodgers, Rickey kept the promise he made 40 years earlier.

Some have argued that Rickey brought Robinson along for personal gain, prestige, and profit. Others say he did it because it was the right thing to do. I suppose it doesn't matter because he got it done, and when has there not been a little greed to go with the balls and strikes in baseball?

The Reds didn't sign any Black players until Chuck Harmon in 1954, but they sort of came close. In 1911, the Reds signed two light-skinned Cubans. When Rafael Almeida and Armando Marasans put on a uniform in the all-White major league, Reds management tried to diffuse the ensuing controversy and announced that the two were as "pure White as Castile soap," referring to one of the popular products of the day. That said a lot to Cincinnatians, who were experts on soap. William Procter and James Gamble formed had formed a soap company in Queen City back in 1837.

Cuban Dolf Luque was picked up by the Reds in July 1918 and would become a great pitcher, known as the "Pride of Havana." The *New York Age*, a Black newspaper founded by Timothy Thomas Fortune, said now that the "the first shock is over, it would not be surprising to see a Cuban a few shades darker.... [I]t would then be easier for colored players who are citizens of this country to get into fast company."

That dream would have to wait a long time in all of baseball and especially Cincinnati. In 1918, Jackie Robinson was just a few months from being born into a family of sharecroppers in Cairo, Georgia. Chuck Harmon wouldn't be born for another eight years. Several clubs came close to signing Black players during that period. Take, for instance, the story of Jimmy Claxton. In May 1916, he pitched one day for the Oakland Oaks of the Pacific Coast League. The owner said he was American Indian. The *San Francisco Call* reported Claxton was "an Indian southpaw." The *San Francisco Chronicle* said, "The Redskin had a nice windup."

He was kicked off the team a few days later when they found out he had African American roots to go with whatever ties he had to Native Americans back in Oklahoma. One report said a jealous teammate complained. Claxton told the *Tacoma News-Tribune* in 1964 he was just told he was no longer part of the team and should turn in his uniform. "No reason was given, but I knew," he said.

An African American would not play in organized, professional baseball for thirty-one years. Claxton later played in the Negro Leagues and was the first African American on a baseball card. He played until he was in his early fifties and died of a heart attack in 1969.

But the answer to the question "why Chuck?" probably can be found in what the world saw in Jackie Robinson. The owners had feared that Black players would cause White fans to stay at home and lose interest in baseball. The Dodgers, however, became even more popular with Robinson, as did Cleveland with Doby.

Like Robinson, Harmon was a college man. There are many other comparisons. Like Robinson, he was very articulate; never a complainer, always hustled, and was easily accepted and liked by his teammates. Chuck agrees that the Reds were hoping to get in Harmon what the Dodgers got in Robinson.

"I paralleled Jackie's background. We both played at White colleges. We were both successful in sports with championships. We kept our nose[s] clean, and we were accountable. They would run a background on you to a T. They would know what you had for breakfast."

The Reds likely checked out Harmon the way the late Roy Campanella said he'd been checked out by the Dodgers. "There was no question I could play [but] did I drink? Did I run around with women? Would I embarrass the club with my conduct? That's what they had to be sure of before they signed any Negro player," Campanella said in 1973, according to the *Baseball Almanac*.

The late Joe Nuxhall was a Reds pitcher when Harmon joined the club in 1954. He told the *Cincinnati Enquirer*'s Tom Groeschen that it didn't take long for Chuck to be comfortable with fans and the team. "I think some guys were apprehensive about it, but that lasted maybe a day," Nuxhall said. "There were some individuals, and I won't mention any names, who were wondering about him. But Charley was such a first-class person that he fit in right away."

If Jackie Robinson got the ball rolling for Blacks in baseball, Willie Mays sent the idea soaring when he exploded on the field for the Giants in 1951. Not only were African Americans showing they could perform, ticket sales were skyrocketing. It's easy to suggest that Mays's popularity put the pressure on other teams. He played in New York, and he was on TV as much as any athlete at the time.

In 1953, the Chicago Cubs and Philadelphia Athletics suited up African Americans. In 1954, along with fans of the Reds, Pittsburgh, Washington, and St. Louis fans got to see Black players on their teams. The Yankees finally came aboard the next year, and by the 1959, all the teams had Black players. Boston was the last team to integrate.

This is probably be a good time to raise our chins, stand up, and step back. Let's take a wide glance at how the world has changed during Chuck's lifetime. It's a nearly ninety-year spectrum filled with benchmarks so symbolic of our lives and culture.

It is a fascinating horizon. Take a longer look. Baseball and America have come a long way, and key benchmarks expand the eighty-plus years Chuck has been on Earth.

From the Babe to Pete
to the Cuban Fireballer

Chuck Harmon's life and times is a wonderful story. His time on earth transcends almost ten decades, from Babe Ruth to Pete Rose to current Reds pitcher Aroldis Chapman.

But before you go any further, and we sure hope you do, let's take care of the least you need to know. That way, if you decide to skip some of the chapters, or spend quality time with the wonderful photographs and statistics we have arranged for you, you will have the basics down. Then, you can read each chapter for more details.

We have included important moments in civil rights history, specifically, those key benchmarks that outlawed racial discrimination. Also, we have inserted great moments in the history of Cincinnati Reds and all of baseball. It's fascinating when you consider America's boiling social cauldron, and all the while Chuck and the other Black players were trying to put it all aside and just play ball. Plenty of White people risked their lives and fortunes to provide Blacks opportunities they otherwise would be denied. That was certainly true of the Cincinnati Reds.

Baseball is such a reflection of America and its struggles for justice. As noted African American author Gerald Early said, in 2,000 years when people study the American civilization, there will be only three things we will be remembered for: the Constitution, jazz, and baseball.

Let's take a quick look at Chuck's life and these parallel snapshots of American history. It seems like Chuck's life and gentlemanly demeanor were never far away from the very best and very worst of human nature. Lets all hope and pray we are better off for what we have struggled to become.

Timeline: 1920–2010

April 14, 1920. The reigning world champion Reds begin their title defense with a 7 to 3 win over the Cubs and famed pitcher Grover Cleveland Alexander. Hoosier Ed Roush becomes the first Red to hit a home run on opening day. Later in the season, eight Chicago White Sox players would be indicted for "fixing" the World Series won by the Reds the previous fall.

May 2, 1920. The Indianapolis ABCs beat the Chicago American Giants, 4 to 2, in the first game of the inaugural season of the Negro National League. It is at the Washington Park in Indianapolis. It has to be played in the Hoosier capital because of the Chicago race riot of 1919. The National Guard was still camped at the Giants diamond at Schorling's Park. During the riots, thirty-eight Blacks were killed and 537 injured. There were race riots in twenty-five cities. Entire neighborhoods were burned and destroyed. Some say this shocking display of White rage led to a demand from African Americans for the equality guaranteed by the Constitution. A new age of confidence for American Blacks was beginning. Marcus Greevey said there should be "No more fear. No more cringing, begging, or pleading."

April 23, 1924. Charles Byron Harmon was born in Washington, Indiana, one of the twelve children of Sherman and Rosa Harmon. Chuck was born near a railroad track in the West End, the Black section of town. He grew up in a cozy home with his siblings and attended a one-room schoolhouse located beside his childhood Methodist church. All three structures still stand today. His father taught school there and was a leader in the church. Even when he was a high-school sports star, he couldn't ride in the same bus with White students. However, Chuck says he holds no grudges or anger. "It's just the way it was then."

Early 1920s. Just fifty miles away from Washington in Evansville, the Ku Klux Klan arrived from Georgia looking for recruits. A Texan named D. C. Stephenson and his disciples preached morality and convinced thousands in Indiana the Klan would keep America ethnically and morally pure.

1925. Stephenson was convicted of kidnapping and sexual assault. Indiana's total Klan membership went from an estimated 350,000 before his arrest to just 15,000 one year later. Now, it's estimated that the Klan has a little more than 40,000 members among America's population of 300 million. Chuck Harmon says that his family was given an opportunity to get ahead and treated with a decent amount of respect. Washington has a history of being a safe haven for African Americans and a community that prides itself on equal opportunity.

1925. The St. Louis Stars were the hit of the Negro National League with phenomenal players like Cool Papa Bell and Willie Wells.

October 8, 1927. The Yankees won 4 to 3 and finished off the Pittsburgh Pirates in four straight World Series games. Babe Ruth hit sixty homers during the season and led New York to 110 wins and just forty-four losses. Forty-seven years, later a Black man by the name of Hank Aaron would receive taunts and death threats as he struggled to break the Babe's records. Waite Hoyt was the leading pitcher for Babe Ruth's Yankees, with a 22–7 record, and later became the Reds radio broadcaster when Chuck Harmon played for Cincinnati. Hoyt retired in 1965 after twenty-four seasons behind the microphone. Despite all those years calling Reds game, Chuck says, psychologically Waite never completely took off those Yankee pinstripes. "He always wanted to talk about the Yankees."

January 15, 1929. Martin Luther King, Jr., is born in Atlanta, Georgia.

April 16, 1929. For the first time, the Reds permit WLW Radio to broadcast more than just the opening game. According to the *Redleg Journal*, compiled by Greg Rhodes and John Snyder, Bob Burdette announced more than forty games that year. Chuck Harmon started listening to baseball on the family's crackling Philco. He mostly remembers hearing the St. Louis Cardinals games.

Did he ever dream of playing with the big league stars? "Are you kidding? There was nothing to dream about. We couldn't play."

March 15, 1930. Washington beats Muncie Central 32 to 21 to win its first state championship in basketball. Chuck Harmon is just five years old when a sports superstar arises in the neighborhood, Dave DeJernett. Playing probably the toughest schedules in the state, DeJernett and Washington High School were a dominant power that was known across the state for years. (The school is still a perennial championship contender, winning its sixth state title in 2010. Chuck Harmon was there to celebrate.) With DeJernett, it is believed this Washington team marked the first time an African American athlete was the star on an integrated, undisputed championship basketball team. Two other athletes before him in New York and Chicago had played in city championships but not in an open state tournament. Newspapers in China reported the event. DeJernett would go on to star for the Harlem Globetrotters.

August 7, 1930. Thomas Shipp and Abram Smith were lynched in Marion, Indiana. The two African Americans had been arrested the night before and charged with murdering a White man and raping his girlfriend. A crowd broke into the jail with sledgehammers and took the men away to be hanged with the help of police and Klan members. The photo of the men hanging from a tree was published around the world. Today, it is believed the two men planned to rob a man but didn't complete the crime. The rape allegation likely was a fabrication.

April 30, 1932. Satchel Paige and Josh Gibson open the season with the Pittsburgh Crawfords. Later in life, Chuck would play with Satchel in exhibition games. "I got to ride in his Cadillac.... I think he was 125 years old at the time," Chuck says with a grin.

October 8, 1939. The Yankees win, 7 to 4, and complete a sweep of the Reds in the World Series.

October 8, 1940. The Reds beat Detroit, 2 to 1, to capture the World Series.

1940–42. Washington, Indiana, and Chuck Harmon enjoy championship seasons. Chuck is an all-sports star in high school, playing football and baseball, but basketball is his main game: He helps lead the Washington Hatchets to back-to-back state titles in 1941 and 1942; all schools in the state of Indiana were in one, huge tournament. One class; one tournament; a single elimination. It is known as March Madness, which today refers to the NCAA men's basketball tournament with its sixty-four teams.

In Chuck's high-school days, there were 777 teams competing in the 1939 tournament, and 769 teams hoping to win it in 1940. Chuck's team swept unblemished twice behind his 524 career points, in front of mostly White and sometimes very angry crowds close to the court. This was nearly twenty years before Jackie Robinson broke the color barrier in Major League Baseball. Although Chuck was one of the top players in the state, Notre Dame, Purdue, and IU did not give scholarships to African Americans. Chuck wanted to play for IU in Bloomington, already a national power in basketball, coached by Branch McCracken. "I wanted to play for Branch, but Branch didn't want me," Chuck says with a laugh. Chuck's Washington High School team played before a crowd of more than 14,000 at each state championship game, a larger audience than many of his games in the major leagues. During his rookie season in 1954, the Reds played before 704,167 fans at the friendly confines of Crosley Field. That's an eighty-one-game average of 8,693 paying customers.

Bill Harmon, who played in the 1941 Indiana high-school basketball championship with his brother Chuck, went to the University of Indianapolis (Indiana Central) and then to work on the railroad. He was transferred to North Vernon, Indiana, just a few miles from Reds owner Powell Crosley's hunting and fishing retreat. Bill started a little construction company. Today it's operated by his sons Bill, Jr., and Tom, and is one of the largest African American construction firms in the nation. Bill, Jr., played for the University of Louisville basketball team. At the 1977 Final Four, his team, coached by Hall of Famer Denny Crum, lost to the University of California, Los Angeles (UCLA), coached by

Hall of Fame coach John Wooden, originally from Martinsville, Indiana. It was Wooden's tenth and final title at UCLA. Tom Harmon played baseball at IU.

The same court where Chuck Harmon played his home games for Washington is where John Wooden played as a visiting player from Martinsville. Actually, Wooden played in the first game at the new gym on November 6, 1925. Martinsville won 47 to 33 in front of 5,200 fans sitting on shiny, new wooden bleachers that cost the community $65,000. That was 1925, and that gym held more people than most college teams average today. It still stands, and the middle school uses it. The "new" basketball palace next door was built in 1966 and seats 7,090. By the way, Wooden's 1926 team would go on to lose in the championship game of Indiana's single-elimination tournament with 719 teams. However, Wooden and the Artesians would win it all in 1927 in a tourney of 731 teams, and lose by one point in the 1928 championship game with 740 schools competing. It sort of makes those odds he faced in winning all those NCAA championships with UCLA against a few dozen other teams seem relatively easy.

Chuck Harmon grew up not far from 1920s Reds star Ed Roush, who is from Oakland City, Indiana. Roush was the first Reds player elected to the National Baseball Hall of Fame in Cooperstown. Roush and Pete Rose were the only Reds to lead the league twice in hitting. Pete did it three times. Chuck's hometown isn't far from that of current Reds star Scott Rolen. He's from Jasper. All three are in the Indiana Baseball Hall of Fame, which is located in Rolen's hometown.

March 21, 1941. Chuck and his Washington Hatchets win the state basketball championship, 39 to 33, over Madison at Hinkle Fieldhouse in Indianapolis. Chuck and his ten teammates are the only team standing of the 777 that began the tournament.

April 14, 1941. Peter Edward Rose is born in Cincinnati. Chuck remembers seeing Pete hanging around the ballpark with his dad.

December 7, 1941. The Japanese attack Pearl Harbor. African Americans are determined to be a part of the war effort, but many are prevented from serving in action.

January 3, 1942. Former Yankee Waite Hoyt is named the Reds radio announcer. Burger Beer is the sponsor. He would be a lifelong friend of his former teammate Babe Ruth and would serve as a pallbearer at the Babe's funeral. Marty Pieratt interviewed Hoyt at his downtown Cincinnati apartment on July 14, 1981. It was the night the All-Star Game was cancelled because of a players' strike. The strike lasted from June 12 to July 31, and the game was eventually played August 10. Portions of the interview, which originally appeared in the *Lawrenceburg Register*, are in this work. Hoyt died August 25, 1984, in Cincinnati while preparing to visit the Hall of Fame in Cooperstown. He had been inducted there in 1969. He is buried in Cincinnati's Spring Grove Cemetery.

March 21, 1942. Chuck Harmon and his Washington High School Hatchets become the fourth school in Indiana history to win consecutive championships. They beat Muncie Burris in a defensive showdown, 24 to 18. The one-class tournament had begun with 769 teams.

January 12, 1943. The Reds announce they will hold spring training at IU in Bloomington until the war is over. The Reds will train in Bloomington for three years before the commissioner allows them to return to Tampa. Because of unpredictable weather, many times the Reds were forced to work out in the field house where the Hoosiers played basketball. The good news is that's where the Reds would discover slugger Ted Kluszewski in 1945, an athlete who was more valuable to IU as a football player than a baseball player. He would go on to be a star first baseman for the Reds from 1947 through 1961.

March, 29, 1943. Chuck plays before more than 18,000 fans at Madison Square Garden in the National Invitational Tournament (NIT) championship basketball game. Recruited by former Washington High School Coach Burl Friddle, Chuck starred for the University of Toledo basketball team as a freshman. The team finished as the NIT national runner-up to St. John's University in 1943, when the NIT arguably was more important than the NCAA tournament. St. John's refused the NCAA bid. Chuck played before a sold-out crowd at Madison Square Garden. Down only six at the half, St. John's pulled away and won, 48 to 27; Chuck scored six points. Before the game, Chuck had the honor of shaking Babe Ruth's hand. He also was named an All-American. Friddle, who coached Washington High School to a state title in 1930, also recruited former Hatchet Art Grove, who had five points in the championship. Harmon would lead Toledo for four years (second-leading scorer three times) letter three times for the Rockets in baseball. By the way, Toledo basketball Coach Friddle still holds some unusual Indiana High School records. He was the only person to play on a state champion (Franklin, 1920) and coach two different champion teams (Washington, 1930), and Ft. Wayne South, 1938).

Using the fake name Charley Fine, Chuck plays in the Negro Leagues for the Indianapolis Clowns. Coach Burl Friddle finds out about this summer job, and Chuck's brief Negro League career comes to an end after one long weekend, five games, and several hot bus rides.

June 10, 1944. Just four days after D-Day, future Harmon teammate Joe Nuxhall becomes the youngest player ever to appear in a major league game in the twentieth century. He is fifteen years, ten months, and eleven days old. The Reds are beaten by St. Louis, 18 to 0, and Nuxhall doesn't pitch again in the big leagues for eight years.

May 14, 1945. Mel Bosser is the winning pitcher as the Reds beat the Phillies, 5 to 4. He'd made the team after showing up at spring training in Bloomington and asking for a tryout. His win comes exactly one week after Germany surrendered in World War II.

June 21, 1945. Japan surrenders at Okinawa. Waite Hoyt goes missing for two days. There are reports that he had amnesia. When Babe Ruth heard about his old friend, he reportedly said that it must have been a new brand of scotch that Waite was drinking. Hoyt admits later that he had problems with alcohol.

April 15, 1947. Baseball's color line is broken as Jack Roosevelt Robinson steps to the plate for the Brooklyn Dodgers. The Negro Leagues began to fade as its players are signed to minor league contracts. The logic of racial segregation will forever be challenged, and the civil rights movement leaps to front of the American political and social conscience.

May 13, 1947. Jackie Robinson makes his first appearance as a Dodger in Cincinnati. He stays with the rest of the team at the Carew Tower's Netherland Plaza Hotel off Fountain Square. However, he is not allowed to use the restaurants or pool. He has a single in four at-bats in the Reds 7 to 5 win. Many in the crowd of 27,164 are Black. There would always be great excitement among African Americans when Jackie came to town, just as there would when Chuck was first called up as Cincinnati's first African American baseball player. Robinson later said Cincinnati was an especially difficult place to play. Despite the excursion trains that carried African Americans from the South to watch him play, his presence led to racial slurs and some death threats.

Summer 1947. Chuck Harmon signs up to play minor league baseball.

1947. IU becomes the first Big Ten school to allow Blacks on its team in 1947, with Bill Garrett of state champion Shelbyville, Indiana.

December 29, 1947. Daurel Pearl Woodley and Charles Bryan Harmon marry in Gloversville, New York, two months after they meet in Toledo, Ohio. Both would say it was "love at first sight."

July 26, 1948. Harry S. Truman declares that there shall be equality among all those who serve in the armed services, no matter what race, color, religion, or national origin.

July 9, 1948. Negro League great Satchel Paige makes his major league debut on the mound for the Cleveland Indians. He is believed to be at least forty-two years old. Chuck would later play in "barnstorming" exhibition games with and against Satch.

August 16, 1948. The great Babe Ruth passes away in New York City, a little more than five years after Chuck Harmon has the opportunity to meet "the Sultan of Swat," a man many scribes have called the best baseball player ever.

1950–53. Chuck Harmon serves in the navy during the Korean War.

1950. Chuck Harmon nearly makes history in the NBA. This is the first year African Americans are allowed to play in the league. Harmon earns a tryout with the Boston Celtics and is told he is the last to be cut by Coach Red Auerbach. However, the truth is very few Blacks would be allowed in the league. Chuck Cooper made it onto the Celtics, the first African American to be drafted out of college. The four players who made it in 1950 were Cooper, Hank DeZonie, Nat "Sweetwater" Clifton and Earl Lloyd. Lloyd became the first Black to enter a NBA game on October 31, 1950; his Washington Capitols took on the Rochester Royals. Cooper, who edged out Harmon on the Celtics roster, became the second Black to play just one day later. Oscar Robertson, whose Crispus Attucks teams won back-to-back Indiana state basketball titles sixteen years after Chuck's Washington Hatchets, entered the league with the Cincinnati Royals in 1960. He is considered to be one of the top fifty players of all time.

1951. The last major league season of the Negro Leagues. The Indianapolis Clowns, a team Chuck played for briefly, are the last professional club of the Negro American League. The Clowns played exhibition games, much like the Harlem Globetrotters, into the 1980s.

Chuck focuses on baseball and is signed to play in the minor leagues, where attitudes are changing about allowing Blacks to play. Chuck is scorching hot for a long time. He hits over the magic mark .300 for five consecutive seasons and is so good the major league teams have to look at him.

April 13, 1954. Four days before Chuck's first appearance with the Reds, Hank Aaron makes his debut with the Milwaukee Braves. He would later best Babe Ruth as the all-time home-run leader. Hank and Chuck remain close friends today. (Two other players became the "first Blacks" for their teams the same day as Aaron: Curt Roberts of the Pittsburgh Pirates and Tom Alson of the St. Louis Cardinals. The Boston Red Sox were the last to integrate, signing Pumpsie Green on July 21, 1959, twelve years and three months after Jackie Robinson's April 15, 1947, debut.)

April 17, 1954. Just shy of his thirtieth birthday, Chuck Harmon becomes the first African American to appear in a regular season game for the Reds. His debut is in Milwaukee as a Cincinnati pinch-hitter in the seventh inning. He pops out, and the Reds lose 5 to 1 to the Braves. Just before Chuck's historic appearance, Nino Escalera, a Puerto Rican of African descent, knocks out a pinch-hit single.

Chuck wears number "10" as a Red. Seven different men wore that number, including one manager, Sparky Anderson, who managed the Big Red Machine to two world championships (1975–76).

Chuck plays for Reds owner Powell Crosley, known as the Henry Ford of radio and a pioneer of compact cars and household appliances. Crosley owned about 4,000 acres in southern Indiana, not far from Chuck's hometown, which he used for hunting and fishing. The land is owned now by the state of Indiana and is known as the Crosley State Fish and Game Preserve.

May 5, 1954. Chuck Harmon leads off and plays third base against Willie Mays and the Giants. Chuck finishes with two hits, Willie only gets one, as the Reds win 7 to 1.

May 7, 1954. Chuck goes two for two against the Cardinals. Stan Musial is hitless as the Reds win 10 to 3.

May 17, 1954. Exactly one month after Chuck Harmon's historic appearance, the Supreme Court rules that segregation of schools is illegal in the *Brown v. the Board of Education of Topeka* decision. It changes America's school system forever and puts civil rights on the front page.

May 30, 1954. Chuck scores the run that makes the difference in the Reds' 6 to 5 victory over Ernie Banks and the Chicago Cubs.

June 22, 1954. Chuck and the Reds beat Jackie Robinson and the Dodgers, 3 to 2, at Ebbets Field.

July 10, 1954. Chuck Harmon hits his first home run off of Warren Spahn. It comes in the third inning, with nobody on and two outs. It is a towering smash to left field. Hank Aaron is held to a triple as the Reds beat the Braves at Crosley Field, 7 to 3.

July 18, 1954. Willie Mays goes three for three, and Chuck goes four for five, as the Reds defeat the Giants, 14 to 4, in the first game of a double header. The Reds lose the second game as Mays hits his thirty-third home run.

July 19, 1954. Chuck leads off the game with a hit as the Reds defeat the Giants, 1 to 0, and go to 47–44 for the season. They look to have an excellent shot at a run for the pennant or at least have the first winning season in ten years, but the club loses fourteen of its next nineteen games. Many times during the second half of the season, Chuck merely pinch hits or doesn't play, even after having outstanding games.

August, 1954. Chuck continues to enjoy his rookie season with the Reds, playing in places like Wrigley Field in Chicago. That same month a fourteen-year-old Chicago kid by the name of Emmett Till visits his family in Mississippi and is beaten, shot, and dumped in the Tallahatchie River for allegedly whistling at a White woman. Two men are arrested but are not convicted by the all-White jury. They later admit their role in the murder in an interview published in *Look* magazine.

September 16, 1954. Despite a two-hit performance by Jackie Robinson, Joe Nuxhall picks up his eleventh win on the mound. Ted Kluszewski hits his forty-ninth home run in a 9 to 3 win over the Dodgers at Ebbets Field. He finishes second to Willie Mays as league MVP.

During Chuck's 1954 season more home runs are hit in Cincinnati's Crosley Field than in any other National League stadium.

April 11, 1955. Chuck hopes for a bright season as the Reds lose the season opener before a crowd of 32,195 at Crosley Field.

July 5, 1955. Reds Manager Birdie Tibbetts and Cardinals Manager Harry Walker have a fight at home plate. After the bench-clearing brawl, the managers realize they are wearing each other's caps. They laugh and hug.

July 23, 1955. Chuck Harmon hits a single with one out in the ninth inning and stops the no-hitter being thrown by New York's Jim Hearn at the Polo Grounds. Chuck receives a death threat and is told he better not play the next game. The FBI is called in, and no incidents are reported. The New York and Cincinnati police and press take the threat very seriously. Chuck later jokes to reporters that it wouldn't be wise to kill him; the Reds were so deep with sluggers they would replace him with somebody better.

1955. Chuck steals nine bases, tying for tenth place in the National League. He does it in only ninety-six games. Four players who finished above him took more than 130 games to steal as many bases, including Hall of Famers Ernie Banks and Duke Snider.

December 1, 1955. Rosa Parks refuses to give up her seat at the front of a public bus in Montgomery, Alabama. Her arrest and the subsequent bus boycott leads to worldwide awareness of the pain and problems of segregation. A young minister by the name of Martin Luther King, Jr., helps organize in the boycott and protests following Mrs. Parks's arrest.

1954–56. Chuck plays on the 1954, 1955, and (for a little while) 1956 Reds teams, which goes down in history as among the most powerful in baseball history, led by a big fellow the Reds discovered on the campus of IU, legendary slugger Ted Kluszewski. During Chuck's rookie year, "Big Klu" became the first Red to lead the league in home runs and RBIs. Some say IU has struggled in football since Ted left. He was a member of the undefeated Big Ten champions in 1945. The Reds discovered Ted during spring training in Bloomington; it was a nice place but not quite the warm springs they later found in Florida and Arizona. If Chuck had not played with so many phenomenal sluggers, he might have had a better career, but he always says he was blessed for all things that happened in his life, even if it meant watching Big Klu belt home runs from the dugout.

Chuck plays in 289 major league games, mostly as a utility infielder. He bats and throws right. In his four seasons with Cincinnati (1954–56), St. Louis (1956–57), and Philadelphia (1957), he bats .238, with seven home runs and fifty-nine RBIs. He plays four seasons of winter baseball in Puerto Rico.

Over the course of his career, Chuck plays with or against such future Hall of Famers as Jackie Robinson, Willie Mays, Hank Aaron, Ernie Banks, Stan Musial, and Roberto Clemente. He plays with most of the other greats of the era, if you include exhibition, barnstorming and spring training games.

The Reds try to be known as the Redlegs during this period because Communists were called Reds, and management didn't like the name association. This is during the "Red Scare" and infamous era of McCarthyism.

Cincinnati is one of the top ten cities in the nation, and the southernmost team. There are no baseball teams in the Deep South or west of St. Louis at this time. When Jackie Robinson comes to town with the Dodgers, African Americans from Ohio, Indiana, Kentucky, and Tennessee come to see him play. It makes the Reds seem like the visiting team. Jackie hangs out with Chuck after some games and one day goes back to Harmon's neighborhood to meet and greet well-wishers.

1956. The house of Dr. Martin Luther King, Jr., is bombed.

April 17, 1956. Frank Robinson makes his major league debut. He will become one of the greatest players of all time in the American and National

Leagues, and the first Black manager in both leagues. At this time, there is an unwritten quota that only so many Blacks can play for each team, usually no more than three.

May 16, 1956. Chuck is traded to the St. Louis Cardinals in exchange for Joe Frazier and Alex Grammas. He is one of the first Blacks to play for the Cards. Tom Alston broke the color barrier there four days before Chuck first played for the Reds in 1954.

May 10, 1957. Chuck is traded by the St. Louis Cardinals to the Philadelphia Phillies for Glen Gorbous. He nearly becomes the first Black to play for the Phillies. He was traded there eighteen days after John Kennedy became the first African American signed by the club, April 22, 1957.

September 25, 1957. The United States federal government sends the message to the world—specifically the state of Arkansas—that it would legally and militarily support integration. After the state's governor tries to prevent nine African American students from attending the all-White Central High School in Little Rock, President Dwight Eisenhower sends 1,000 paratroopers and 10,000 national guard soldiers to ensure the Supreme Court's equal school decision will be obeyed.

1957. Chuck hangs up his spikes and goes to work for McGregor Sporting Goods. There, he helps convince many of the great players, including Willie Mays, to use the equipment he was selling.

1960. As Chuck adjusts to life after playing baseball, America is adjusting to a new, more equal way of life. On February 1, 1960, the first of many "sit-ins" brings attention to discrimination at restaurants and lunch counters. By 1961, there are similar demonstrations throughout the South and Midwest.

1961. Freedom Rides highlight segregation aboard buses, in bus terminals and restrooms, and at water fountains. Violence and KKK involvement are the result in Alabama. Black riders are arrested in Jackson, Mississippi, after they use Whites-only restrooms.

July 17, 1961. Ty Cobb passes away and is buried in a crypt near his hometown of Royston, Georgia. Known as one of the meanest and most aggressive players ever, Cobb also has the highest batting average ever: .367. Pete Rose eventually passes him in number of hits. Cobb was vehemently opposed to Blacks playing in the major leagues. Local press accounts suggest that while 400 people showed up at his funeral, most of them were little leaguers who were told to attend. Only three of his former teammates showed up.

August 4, 1961. Barack Obama is born at Kapi'olani Medical Center for Women and Children in Honolulu, Hawaii. His parents, Barack Obama, Sr. and Ann Dunham, met at the University of Hawaii. His mother's ancestors settled in Tipton County, Indiana, in the 1850s. The farmhouse owned by Jacob and Louisa Dunham still stands today.

October 1, 1962. After a bitter fight with the governor of Mississippi, James Meredith wins a lawsuit and becomes the first African American to enter University of Mississippi. Escorted by U.S. marshals, Meredith walks onto the campus on September 30, 1962. In violence that follows, two people are killed, twenty-eight marshals suffer gunshot wounds, and as many 160 people are injured. President Kennedy sends troops to the campus to stop the violence. The next day Meredith goes to class. (He later became a professor at the University of Cincinnati. His wife, Judy, was a reporter for the NBC affiliate, WLWT Channel 5.)

Spring training, 1963. The Reds are playing the New York Yankees in Tampa. Mickey Mantle says he hit a home run about 460 feet over the fence. A young rookie named Pete Rose slams against the fence as if he had a chance to catch it. Mantle says the ball was 100 feet over Rose's head and still rising. Teammate Whitey Ford reportedly says, "Mick, you see 'ole Charlie Hustle out there trying to catch that ball." The name stuck to Pete.

Spring and summer, 1963. Reverend Fred Shuttlesworth fights for the release of civil rights protesters in Alabama. On June 11, Governor George Wallace tries to block Blacks from entering the University of Alabama. President John F. Kennedy considers federalizing the Alabama National Guard. On September 15, the Sixteenth Street Baptist Church in Birmingham is bombed, killing four young girls. On the evening of June 12, President Kennedy addresses the nation via TV and radio, pleading for respect for equal rights. The next day Black activist Medgar Evers is murdered in Mississippi. One week later, President Kennedy submits his civil rights bill to Congress. Reverend Fred Shuttlesworth becomes a prominent, long-time minister in Cincinnati.

August 28, 1963. Two-hundred thousand people march on Washington, D.C., protesting discrimination. Dr. Martin Luther King, Jr., delivers his famous "I Have a Dream" speech.

November 22, 1963. President Kennedy is assassinated in Dallas. He had inflamed many in America with his demands for social justice.

July 2, 1964. The Civil Rights Act, banning discrimination based on "race, color, religion, or national origin," is enacted by Congress.

August 4, 1964. Three civil rights workers—one Black, two White—are murdered in Mississippi. They had been trying to register Black voters and went to investigate the burning of a Black church. They were arrested by police for speeding, and later turned over to members of the KKK. They were never seen alive again.

During the 1964 season, Boston's Red Auerbach puts five Black starters on the NBA court for the first time.

1964. Dr. Martin Luther King, Jr., is awarded the Nobel Peace Prize.

April 9, 1965. The Colt .45s become the Houston Astros and move into the brand new Astrodome, a covered stadium. An artificial grass known as Astroturf is born. The Reds will play on the same kind of carpet five years later at the new Riverfront Stadium.

1965. The Voting Rights Act of 1965 restores and protects voting rights. When President Johnson signs the bill that President Kennedy had so tirelessly pushed, it becomes the most sweeping civil rights legislation in U.S. history.

November 13, 1965. Branch Rickey checks himself out of a St. Louis hospital and drives about 125 miles to Columbia, Missouri for a speaking engagement. Leaning on his cane, he tells the crowd, "I'm going to tell you a story out of the Bible about spiritual courage." Then he says he cannot continue. He collapses and never speaks again. Attending his funeral are both Jackie Robinson and Bobby Bragan, who had opposed Jackie joining the team in 1947. Bragan says he came because Branch Rickey made him a better man.

December 12, 1965. On the day Branch Rickey dies, the second Black Red and the team's first star, Frank Robinson, is let go. He had been an amazing star, hitting a record thirty-eight home runs as a rookie, and earning the National League MVP award in 1961. Cincinnati may think he is too old at thirty, but he is not. He goes to Baltimore and becomes the only player to win an MVP award in both leagues.

March 5, 1966. Marvin Miller is hired to head the player's union. The showdown to decide who would control baseball—owners or players—begins. Miller helps players increase minimum salaries and pensions. The minimum salary in 1946 was $5,000. Twenty years later, it had increased by only $2,000. Miller helped rid the league of the reserve clause that bound players to their original teams, which some thought it sounded an awful lot like slavery.

March 19, 1966. Texas Western coach Don Haskins starts five Black players for the first time in NCAA basketball championship history and defeats an all-White Kentucky team coached by Adolph Rupp, 72 to 65. Haskins' childhood friend, Herman Carr, an African American, influenced his life. The story of Texas Western (now the University of Texas at El Paso) was the basis for the movie *Glory Road*.

June 6, 1966. Civil rights leader James Meredith is shot during a voting rights march from Memphis, Tennessee, to Jackson, Mississippi. He survives. In

2002, his son Joseph is named the top doctoral student in the University of Mississippi School of Business, the same school that had tried to stop his dad from entering, thus becoming a flash point for the civil rights movement.

July 25, 1966. Boston's Ted Williams is inducted into the Hall of Fame at Cooperstown, New York. He tells reporters, "Baseball gives every American boy a chance to excel.... I hope someday Satchel Paige and Josh Gibson can be added here in some way as a symbol of great Negro League ballplayers. They are not here only because they did not get a chance."

September 30, 1967. Hannah Milhous Nixon passes away. The mother of future President Richard Nixon, she was born March 7, 1885, just outside of Butlerville, Indiana, a village settled by Quakers from Butlerville, Ohio. In both regions, Quakers were known for providing safe havens for African Americans along the Underground Railroad. Near her birthplace, the Harmon family operates one of the largest African American–owned construction and steel companies in the United States.

1967. Chuck Harmon buys a service station in Indianapolis to help bolster his family income. It is located near Crispus Attucks High School, a school designed by Klan sympathizers to keep Blacks segregated. Crispus Attucks becomes a great institution with many Black college professors serving as its teachers. It is where Oscar Robertson, the future Indiana and world basketball legend, first competes in the nearby streets and on the playgrounds.

April 4, 1968. Martin Luther King, Jr., is shot to death in Memphis. That night in Indianapolis, not far from Crispus Attucks High School and Chuck's business, Robert F. Kennedy, the front-runner in the current presidential campaign, informs a mostly Black crowd that King has been killed. Reportedly, Kennedy had been told by police to avoid this "dangerous ghetto," but he did not listen. He tells the crowd to emulate King and his passion for non-violence, that "Martin Luther King dedicated his life to love and to justice between fellow human beings. He died in the cause of that effort.... What we need is not division, not hatred [but] love and wisdom, and compassion toward one another. Say a prayer for our country and our people." Indianapolis is the only major city in the United States that is riot free on the night Dr. King died.

April 11, 1968. Just a week after Dr. King is killed, President Lyndon Johnson signs the Civil Rights Act of 1968, prohibiting discrimination in the sale, rental, or financing of housing.

June 5, 1968. Senator Robert Kennedy is assassinated just after midnight following a celebration of his California primary victory. Rosemary Clooney, famed singer from the Cincinnati area and aunt of actor George Clooney, is present in the ballroom when Kennedy is shot in the nearby pantry. She soon suffers a nervous breakdown.

September 25, 1969. Satchel Paige makes his last major league appearance, pitching for the Kansas City Athletics. He is believed to be at least fifty-nine, although he could have been fifty-five, sixty-six, or maybe even seventy-two. Chuck says his old friend might have been over 100, but he says it with a smile.

October 10, 1970. Gary, Indiana's Jackson Five sing the national anthem at the first game of the World Series at Riverfront. The Reds faced the Orioles. It was the first World Series game played on Astroturf. The Orioles won, 4 to 3.

October 15, 1970. The Baltimore Orioles defeat the Reds and win the World Series four games to one behind the power of Frank Robinson and amazing play from Brooks Robinson at third base. It was the last series played entirely in the daytime.

Along with his work with McGregor and his small business in Indianapolis, Chuck works as a scout for the Cleveland Indians and Atlanta Braves. He serves in the same capacity for the Indiana Pacers of the NBA. He later goes to work for the Hamilton County Judicial system, working in downtown Cincinnati at the courthouse.

June 18, 1972. The Supreme Court votes 5 to 3 against Curt Flood, who had refused to be traded from the Cardinals to the Phillies saying, "By God, this is America, and I'm a human being.... I do not feel like I am a piece of property to be bought and sold." Flood said the reserve clause binding him to his original team violated the Thirteenth Amendment abolishing slavery, that people in Vietnam were dying for the rights he didn't have in his chosen profession. Jackie Robinson testified on his behalf. The Supreme Court disagreed and sided with the owners. Flood never played baseball again. Chuck had been housed with Curt Flood and other Black players during spring training in the 1950s.

October 14, 1972. Jackie Robinson throws out the ceremonial first pitch in Cincinnati as the Reds open the series with Oakland. He tells the crowd at Riverfront Stadium that he will be happier when he sees a "Black face" coaching in Major League Baseball. Johnny Bench catches the ball and returns it to the legendary player; the two exchange a few friendly words.

October 24, 1972, Jackie Robinson dies of a heart attack and complications related to diabetes at his home in Stamford, Connecticut. He was 53. Nearly 3,000 people showed up for his funeral. Reverend Jesse Jackson speaks at the services. He says, "Jackie Robinson stole home … and he's safe." Dodger sportscaster Red Barber says Robinson died from the load he had to bear. Three days later, Frank Robinson is named the first Black manager in the American League. He became a player-manager for the Cleveland Indians. He would later become the first Black manager in the National League when the San Francisco Giants hired him in 1981.

October 22, 1972. The Reds lose 3 to 2 against the Oakland A's in the seventh game of the World Series at Riverfront Stadium.

December 31, 1972. Pittsburgh Pirates star Roberto Clemente dies in a plane crash while on his way to help earthquake victims in Nicaragua. He had encountered pressure because of his Puerto Rican and African heritage, but Pittsburgh came to love him. At the time of his death, he was one of eleven players with 3,000 or more hits.

During the 1972–73 seasons, Chuck's nephew Billy is one of the top high-school recruits in the nation along with teammate Danny Brown at Jennings

County High School in North Vernon, Indiana. The close friends both decide to play for the University of Louisville. Most years, the Indiana All-Star team has twelve players. In Billy's senior year they decided to take only eleven. Danny Brown makes the team. Billy Harmon, who scored more points, is denied with no reason given.

April 4, 1974. On opening day in Cincinnati, Hank Aaron of the Atlanta Braves homers to tie Babe Ruth's all-time home-run mark of 714. Four days later, he passes the Babe with a shot in Atlanta. Along the way, he survives the pressure and death threats, along with hateful letters and racial slurs from the stands. He goes from the hugs of his teammates into the arms of his mother and father, Herbert Sr. and Estella Aaron.

October 21, 1975. Game six of the World Series between the Reds and Boston is called maybe the best game ever. Carlton Fisk wins the dramatic seesaw contest in the bottom of the twelfth with a home run, but the next night the Reds bring the world championship trophy back to Cincinnati with a come-from-behind 4 to 3 victory. Seventy-five million viewers, the most ever to watch a sporting event on television, watch that game.

December 23, 1975. Baseball's reserve clause is overturned in court. Owners no longer can hold players to their original team. What Curt Flood compared to slavery is no longer the case. The era of free agency and multi-million-dollar contracts begins.

October 21, 1976. The Reds sweep the Yankees and win the World Series. The ball club is regarded as one of the best ever. The Reds have eight All-Star candidates: Pete Rose, Johnny Bench, Ken Griffey, Joe Morgan, Tony Perez, George Foster, Dave Concepcion, and Cesar Geronimo.

May 29, 1977. A grief-stricken Tristate escapes with Marty and Joe on the radio and hears the call of a Reds 8 to 1 win over the Dodgers in Los Angeles. Just one day earlier, 164 people had died a few miles from Riverfront Stadium in a fire at the Beverly Hills Supper Club.

May 5, 1978. Pete Rose knocks his 3,000th hit in a loss to the Expos, 4 to 3. Playing first base for Montreal is Pete's buddy and former Red Tony Perez

October 17, 1979. In the mid-1970s, the Pittsburgh Pirates put together the first all-Black and Hispanic team. Eventually, they surprise the Reds in the playoffs and beat the Orioles for a World Series title.

June 8, 1982. Satchel Paige passes away in Kansas City, Missouri. He is believed to be at least seventy-five. Some say he could still throw the ball as hard as some big leaguers.

November 2, 1983. Martin Luther King, Jr., Day is declared a national holiday as President Ronald Reagan signs the bill proposed by Congresswoman Katie Hall of Indiana. Six million signatures were collected for the petition to Congress, believed to be the most ever.

August 15, 1984. The Reds announce Pete Rose is coming home to play and manage. Having known Pete since he was a kid hanging around Crosley Field, Chuck Harmon is extremely pleased.

December 21, 1984. Marge Schott purchases the majority interest in the Reds.

September 11, 1985, Pete Rose breaks Ty Cobb's all-time hit mark with hit number 4,192.

January 20, 1986. The Martin Luther King, Jr., Day federal holiday is observed for the first time.

August 17, 1986. Player-manager Pete Rose bats for the last time and is struck out by San Diego's Goose Gossage. He leaves after playing in 3,562 games, batting 14,035 times, and knocking 4,256 hits—all records.

1989. A tough year for all fans of baseball, but especially for those who live in Cincinnati and visit the Reds' clubhouse and stands. For the whole season, the national spotlight is on the gambling investigation of manager Pete Rose. One week after he suspends Rose for life, Major League Baseball Commissioner Bart Giamatti suddenly dies of a heart attack. Then an earthquake occurs during the World Series at San Francisco.

April 20, 1990. Rose pleads guilty to filing false income-tax returns.

August 8, 1990. Rose begins serving his five-month sentence at the Federal Prison in Marion, Illinois.

October 16, 1990. The Reds' Eric Davis homers in his first World Series at bat. The Reds, mostly a team Pete Rose had built, goes on to sweep the Oakland Athletics in four games, considered one of the biggest upsets in baseball history. On Saturday, October 20, Davis injures his kidney hustling for a ball in the first inning of game 4. He is outwardly bitter about his treatment by the Reds following his injury, saying he was left back in Oakland and implying that he was treated differently because he is Black. Chuck Harmon begins to be recognized for being the first Black Red. Reds owner Marge Schott emphatically denies ever having racist feelings.

January 7, 1991. Rose is released from prison and begins 1,000 hours of community service.

April 29, 1992. The first race riots in decades break out in Los Angeles after a jury acquits four White police officers for the videotaped beating of African American Rodney King.

October 24, 1992. The Toronto Blue Jays win the first World Series played outside the United States. The manager is a Black man from San Antonio, Texas, Clarence Gaston, called "Cito" after a Mexican-American wrestler he liked when he was a kid. The first-ever African American to manage a World Series championship team does it again in 1993. He had been Hank Aaron's roommate when they both played at Atlanta. According to an article in the March 1994 issue of *Ebony* magazine, Gaston said Aaron taught him how to be a man and stand on his own.

April 9, 2001. Downtown Cincinnati is the scene of riots and violence, which reach a boiling point after fifteen Black males under the age of forty are killed by police or die in custody. Investigations and trials follow. No serious incidents have been reported since the three-day crisis.

March 28, 2003. Chuck Harmon throws out the "first pitch ever" at the new Great American Ballpark in an exhibition game between the Reds and the Cleveland Indians.

March 31, 2003. Former President George H.W. Bush throws out the first pitch of a regular season game at Great American. He fills in for his son, the then current president, who could not make it. Pittsburgh defeats the Reds, 10 to 1. The younger Bush gets his chance a few years later. On April 3, 2006, President George W. Bush becomes the first president to throw out a ceremonial first pitch on opening day in Cincinnati.

June 23, 2003. The Supreme Court upholds the University of Michigan Law School's policy of considering race in selecting students for a diverse student body

April 2004. A plaque with Chuck Harmon's image and accomplishment as the first African American to play for the Reds is mounted near the main entrance to Great American Ball Park. Chuck usually passes it on his way to the parking lot underneath the stadium. The plaque was dedicated during Chuck Harmon Recognition night at Great American honoring the fiftieth anniversary of his debut.

October 31, 2004. President Bush holds a rally at Great American Ballpark just days before his narrow victory over Senator John Kerry. Most political experts say it is this region of Ohio that puts Bush over the top.

October 24, 2005. Rosa Parks passes away.

January 30, 2006. Coretta Scott King passes away.

November 2, 2008. Barack Obama is elected the first African American president of the United States.

June 20, 2009. At the 2009 Civil Rights Game in Cincinnati, former President Bill Clinton honors Chuck in his speech.

In the decade leading up to the 2010 season, Chuck attends more games than any veteran Reds player. His four season tickets are worth more than the Reds paid him when he played. One of the former players to sit and chat with Chuck late in the 2009 season was the all-time hit king, Pete Rose.

Chuck Harmon still lives in the Golf Manor neighborhood of Cincinnati. Six blocks of Rosedale Avenue near his home were renamed Chuck Harmon Way.

November 28, 2009. His beloved wife, Daurel Pearl Harmon, dies at their home two days before her eighty-third birthday. It was one month and one day shy of their sixty-second wedding anniversary. After the Saturday, December 5, memorial service for Pearl, Chuck tries to lift his spirits by visiting with more than 17,000 friends and baseball fanatics at the annual Redsfest in downtown Cincinnati.

January 2010. Chuck's high school honors him before the Hatchets victory. Nearly 7,000 fans give him a standing ovation, and he signs more than 100 autographs that weekend and poses for dozens of pictures. The team plays in a field house that seats 7,100. The gym where Chuck played is now used by the middle school. He shoots buckets during the team's Saturday morning practice.

March 27, 2010. Chuck is honored at Conseco Fieldhouse in Indianapolis along with all living former state champions. His high-school alma mater, Washington, wins its sixth straight title.

April 5, 2010. Chuck attends opening day, the Reds versus St. Louis. He had played for both of those teams in his career. Cardinal Albert Puhouls has a monster day with two home runs and four hits total. Scott Rolen, from Jasper, Indiana, hits a homer for the Reds.

May 15, 2010. Chuck is honored again by his beloved Reds organization during Major League Baseball's civil rights game between Cincinnati and the St. Louis Cardinals. This day is called "Chuck Harmon Day." The Reds give away 30,000 number "10" Harmon jerseys.

Tons of numbers, myriad dates. It all sort of blurs now when Chuck reminisces. But there is one thing that brings him to complete focus, presence, and authenticity: the Pearl of his life, the best chapter in his life. Marrying her, he says, was his greatest accomplishment.

Pearl, My Girl

Many White people will never understand what Black people had to go through before the Civil Rights Act, or even after it was enacted: the pain, the anguish, the deep anger associated with racism and segregation.

Think about this for a moment. Pearl, Chuck Harmon's wife, wanted to see her husband play in Tulsa, the home of one of the Cincinnati Reds' minor league teams in the 1950s. It was her first visit to the minor league park. Pearl was so light skinned many people didn't realize she was part African American. She is blonde and about as multicultural as a person can get, part French, Irish, Indian, and African.

The team management couldn't decide whether to let her sit by the other players' wives or make her sit in the "Negro" section. They called the Cincinnati front office. The powers that be in the Queen City said to make sure the Harmons didn't leave. They had big plans for Chuck.

Pearl said she would do whatever it took to make Chuck the only Black player on the team. She wanted her man to be successful, even if she had to use a ballpark outhouse where other Blacks were forced to go. Recalling that time, Chuck said, "It hurts.... You just say, 'One of these days, things are going to get better.'" They did, thanks in a large part to Pearl and Chuck.

Chuck Harmon is the first to say he has lived a glorious life. That's not just because he was the first African American to play for the Reds in the team's long and storied history, or because he is mentioned in the same breath as Jackie Robinson in speeches given by such luminaries as former President Bill Clinton in 2009. No, his redemption comes from his family—his mom and dad and the eight sisters and three brothers he grew up with in a cozy one-and-a-half story home at the corner of 16th and Maxwell in Washington, Indiana. His mother Rosa and father Sherman did a wonderful job with their dozen darlings: boys Sherman Jr., Bill, and Chuck, and girls Millicent, Farrel, Joyce, Rose, Savannah, Ruth, Josephine, Jean, and Lois. All but one earned college degrees. Joyce, Savannah, Rose, and Chuck still walk this Earth.

His mom, dad, brothers, and sisters were always there for him, a built-in cheering section. But for most of his adult life, Chuck's foundation was his wife, Pearl, and their children Charlene, Chuck Jr., and Cheryl. The kids have been gone from home longer than the years since the last time the Reds won the World Series. But they are still his pride and joy, much more than any trophies, championships, or first anything could ever be. Family "is the most important thing in life," Chuck says.

The feeling is mutual. Just ask Chuck, Jr., a top-notch athlete who was successful at the high-school and college levels. "My mother and father have been great role models and inspirations for me," he says. "They have always been there for me, any time or day. I love them for being the best parents you can have. They always wanted the best for me and my sisters.... I really miss my mom, being a mamma's boy."

The one enduring thing about Chuck Harmon's life was Daurel Pearl Harmon. That's why it was so hard for him to let her go as she slipped away on Saturday, November 28, 2009. She died in her bed, uncomplaining, despite the cancer that slowly consumed her. A New York gal, she was happy to see on her bedroom TV those darn Yankees win another World Series. Whatever baseball team Chuck played for was her favorite; after that, it was always the Yankees.

She died at the home on Harmon Drive they shared for decades, surrounded by Chuck and her family. Chuck feels like the street was named for both of them, not just him. He had heard the cheers and jeers of millions, but now Chuck's biggest fan was silent.

Pearl's memorial service took place Saturday, December 5, 2009, at Crossroad Community Church, just a couple of parking lots away from

Cincinnati Gardens. That's where the great Oscar Robertson played for the Cincinnati Royals en route to the NBA Hall of Fame, and just across the street from where General Motors made Camaros until they shipped the process overseas.

It was a cloudless, sunny day in Cincinnati, yet the temperatures hovered around freezing for most of the day. On television, the University of Cincinnati football team was in the unlikely position of flirting with a national title while putting its 9–0 record on the line against the University of Pittsburgh. On the streets downtown, Bengal fans were once again proud to wear orange and Black. Many fans were already starting to gear up for the next day's game against the Detroit Lions at Paul Brown Stadium. Cincinnati's NFL team was headed back to the playoffs after a long drought. But don't be confused about this football talk. Cincinnati is as much a baseball town as any could be.

In 1869, a few years after the Civil War ended, the Cincinnati Red Stockings became the first organized, professional baseball team. They went 124–6 in their first two seasons. Baseball flows in the veins of this river city; it always has and likely always will. Just visit on opening day sometime. It's a jolly holiday. Hope will always spring eternal when it comes to baseball in Cincinnati.

For example, on the December day when Chuck said goodbye to Pearl, about 140 years after the birth of Cincinnati baseball, when football in the Buckeye State would seemingly take first place, nearly 20,000 baseball fans were jammed into the convention center.

It was Redsfest, a two-day celebration of Cincinnati baseball—past, present, and future. A sad but resolute Chuck Harmon was one of the former players there to sign autographs. He said goodbye to Pearl, his friends, and his family and went downtown to once again be a Cincinnati Red.

Amid tears at the funeral service, their daughter Cheryl Harmon said, "We better get going, Mom wouldn't want Dad to be late." Chuck hardly said a word at the service. He sat with his head bowed and tears in his eyes. Pearl was his number one fan, coach, and teammate and was there beside him on the bench of life for sixty-two years, cheering him on.

Just a few weeks earlier she had been diagnosed with pancreatic cancer. Chuck would sit by her side and hold her hand. Sometimes at night the family would see Chuck standing over her bed.

Chuck's nephew, Bill Harmon, said Pearl had it tougher in many ways than Chuck. "Can you imagine what it was like for her?" he asked at the service. "She had to sit in the stands and hear the murmurs. He could go out there and hit and run and field and forget about it. She was there in the stands."

There were moments when she didn't feel comfortable sitting with other players' wives. She was light skinned, but darker than they were and married to an African American. Ushers often were confused about where to put her. It was so frustrating at times that she would just go back to the car and listen to the game on the radio. In the car or in the seats, Pearl was always Chuck's biggest fan, and he always played more for her than any teammate, manager, or owner.

There were many good times and many uncomfortable situations. Just like Chuck—sometimes in the majors and just about always in the minors— she would have to stay in different hotels and eat at different restaurants. Because of the lighter color of her skin, even Black players' wives didn't feel comfortable being with her at times.

Cheryl Harmon recalls her mom and dad arriving at school to pick her up after an athletic event, decked out in formal attire. They had just attended Hall of Fame catcher Johnny Bench's wedding. "One of the kids said, 'I didn't know your mom was White,'" she remembers. Pearl wasn't White; she was of mixed heritage. She always moved past awkward comments with style, grace, and the support of her husband.

Chuck Harmon played four years in the big leagues with the Reds, St. Louis Cardinals, and Philadelphia Phillies and nearly fifteen total seasons of professional baseball. Yet he was lucky to earn $5,000 to $10,000 a year in those days. Today, he would possibly make $1 million annually and be more like Derek Jeter with a personal trainer, chef, publicist, and agent. But Chuck had all those in one—Pearl.

"He had that for sixty-two years," said son-in-law Patrick Edmond. "It was unchallenged and unreal love."

At the service, as her pictures were shown and Nat King Cole's "Unforgettable" played, friends and family couldn't say enough about their devotion toward each other. "No man ever loved a woman like my uncle loved Aunt Fuzz," Bill Harmon said. "It teaches me how to love my wife. I want to be just like you."

The Harmons have much to be proud of, but Pearl's family had stories to tell, too. Friend Bob Mitchell says her family was originally from Madagascar. "The family settled in upstate New York. She had ancestors who set the table for George Washington. Many of her relatives were part of the abolition movement. They were on Broadway as minstrels," Mitchell said.

During World War II, she had one brother in the "White" navy and one brother in the "Black" navy. When Pearl was asked if she was Black or White, she would just say "international."

Pearl wanted to work in the New York fashion world. She was attending Syracuse University when she met Chuck, who was playing in the minor leagues at the time. She gave up her career to be a loving wife and mother. "She was as near a perfect person as I ever seen," Mitchell added. "She was so kind, so gentle, so unbelievably honest. She was everything … and Chuck and Pearl, I think it was the greatest love affair I have ever seen."

The family joked that during Chuck's playing days, when Jackie Robinson and the Dodgers came to town, Chuck would call home and let Pearl know that Jackie may need a bite to eat and a place to stay. There is some kind of wonderful sadness in the thought of an iconic figure in American history sleeping on Chuck's couch and eating whatever Pearl had to fix because he was not welcome in restaurants and hotels. It also shows you that, from minor leagues to the majors to the final innings of life, Chuck and Pearl were a team.

Here's a poem he wrote for her about twenty years ago when they started having grandchildren.

To Pearl

There was a special year, the 26th, I remember
And on the day, she was born, the 30th of November
She came into this world crying, so soft and oh so cuddly,
Her parents were so very proud that Dad brought out the bubbly!

As years went past and she grew older, a beauty she became,
Along with Charles with big broad shoulders; then Harmon was her name.
Their marriage took place on the 29th, on a cold December,
Toledo, Ohio, was the place, and a day I'll always remember.

With hair of blonde and eyes of pearl, in 1947,
I always knew she would be my girl.
A marriage made in heaven!
A baseball fan she grew to be, her man was Number One,
She followed him through thick and thin, they had a lot of fun!

She cooks and sews and cleans the house, her chores from day-to-day.
I'm very proud to be her spouse, a price I'm glad to pay!
Our household grew from two to three when Charlene was born.
The only birth when I was home; sound the trumpets and the horn!
Upon my knee, she did sit, so playful and so bright.
I always knew she would be a hit because she was such a sight!
And them along came our son, Charlie is his name.
And though our hearts she had won, we loved him just the same.

It wasn't too much long after that along came Cheryl Jean.
With curly hair and eyes of brown, the prettiest baby ever seen.
So here we are with our three kids, now grown and on their own.
With Dani and Justin and Bridget, too, it's such a happy home!

As long as there's a god in heaven, our marriage it will last.
And now the lucky number's seven, our family has grown so fast.
After forty years I never made it to the baseball Hall of Fame,
But being married to Daurel Pearl makes living all the same!

According to family friend Tony Williams, a couple of years ago Pearl said, "I've always wondered what opportunities Chuck would have had, had he not married me." Yet Williams said, and Pearl agreed, that looking like a mixed-race couple didn't matter to them. They had the love.

Life for Chuck has been tough in the days since Pearl's departure. He still lives in their same home, but it's not the same. Chuck had his "man cave" in the basement, surrounded by pictures, trophies, and mementos. At the top of the stairs, just around the corner would be Pearl. She would calmly sit in her chair, waiting for Chuck to meet for a bite to eat or conversation, something they had been doing since Dwight Eisenhower was president and Elvis Presley was just beginning to shake, rattle, and roll.

Chuck's grandson stays with him and keeps him company, talking about sports and the next public appearance for this beloved old Red. His children and friends try to help out and keep him thinking about something, anything, rather than the ache in his heart for the Pearl of his life.

But he still talks about her, in the present tense, as if she is still there. Perhaps she still is.

Back Home Again in Indiana

Chuck Harmon knew he had been a lucky man. It was March 27, 2010. He was nearing his eighty-sixth birthday. He was back in Indiana where his life had begun.

As he stood beside a basketball court filled with about 17,000 people, it kind of all fit together for him. It was the 100th annual Indiana basketball tournament. The finals are now played at Conseco Fieldhouse, where the Indiana Pacers of the NBA play. They used to be played at Hinkle Fieldhouse across town, where America's 2010 Butler team plays. That also was where Chuck was undefeated in basketball tournament play.

On this night, Chuck was being honored at halftime as one of the greatest players of all-time, along with Oscar Robertson and Larry Bird. Even better, his beloved high school, Washington, was winning its sixth title. Chuck's teams had won two, and he wanted to see the young boys he had befriended win the last of a championship six-pack.

He stood silent. The crowd was silent. The lights went down. The spotlight came on. It was shining on Chuck Harmon. He was the first all-time great to be called out on the court to a standing ovation. He took off his Cincinnati Reds cap and waved to the crowd. "I don't know why I was called first. But it was great. It was wonderful," he says.

The icing on the cake: Washington won 65 to 62 in overtime against Gary Wallace. Chuck could sleep well. Like so many times in his life, he felt like a winner.

Chuck had renewed his ties with old school and hometown a few months earlier.

Chuck Harmon had many, many good days in his time on Earth. But with Pearl's death still a very fresh wound on his heart, Chuck needed a little something else to think about. Going home, he thought, might just do the trick. Homecoming night was coming up at Washington High School. They wanted to honor Chuck before a big rivalry game with Booneville.

So Chuck and his daughter, Cheryl, drove the nearly four hours from Cincinnati to Davies County, Indiana. River Road near Great American Ballpark in Cincinnati turns into U.S. 50 just west of downtown. Stay on it for about 200 miles, and you'll end up a few blocks from Chuck's old high school.

Not far off the highway's beaten path you will find Allen Field, where he played football and baseball. Washington kids started playing ball there in 1909. It's still being used today. The place where he played basketball is still around, too. It's called the Hatchet House. With sweat, skill, and determination, these are the places where Chuck learned what it took to be a winner.

The basketball arena is really too special to be called a gym. It officially seats 7,090. It was built for basketball in 1966 and has mostly wooden seats in an arena style. It had the wooden floor bleachers from the 1925 gym until a recent remodeling. This place is basketball. It looks, smells, and feels like basketball. Close your eyes and you can hear the shoe squeaks, grunts, and deafening cheers. You can smell that popcorn.

It was Friday, January 29, 2010. Chuck was coming home, and it felt really, really, good. "Ah, it feels good to be back," he said as he stood near a tunnel leading to the Hatchet House.

They sat Chuck so close to the court his long arms might have been used for some Hatchet defense. Before any sort of announcement was made, folks began lining up for an autograph, to shake his hand, or give him a hug.

Old-timers remembered his athletic ability and sportsmanship. And like Reds fans would later, they remembered his quickness.

But there was so much more to this guy. He was a gentleman on and off the court or field of competition. When you see how Chuck's character was built, you understand why manager Birdie Tebbetts chose him for the Reds. Tebbetts was a thinking man. He was a philosophy major who graduated with honors from Providence College in 1934. The thinking worked. Tebbetts, Harmon, and the 1954 Reds had the best Cincinnati record in ten years.

Back to the future.

Several youngsters asked Chuck to sign the backs of their shirts. One man, who had been in Chuck's class, showed up wearing the high-school letter on his sweater he wore when Chuck played with the Hatchets.

Before the national anthem, the crowd gave Chuck a standing ovation as his accomplishments in life were read aloud. The applause grew, and then Chuck waved his Reds cap to the crowd and gave a double thumbs up to the young boys standing just a few feet away in Hatchet uniforms. It was quite a homecoming. Once a star in Washington, Indiana, always a star in Washington, Indiana. Chuck may not have worn a Hatchet jersey for more than a half century, but he was treated like he'd graduated with the previous year's champions.

If you like high-school basketball, or maybe just the feel and emotion of a small town that is completely united about something, pay Washington, Indiana, a visit on game night. That is, if you can get a ticket. It's a city of about 12,000; it actually had a few thousand more when Chuck was there. Right now his old school has an enrollment of 760. There were about 1,000 students when Chuck walked the halls.

Washington is an hour from Evansville, an hour and twenty minutes from Terre Haute, and a quick thirty-five minutes from the Illinois border. The city is mostly White, with only a few hundred African Americans; in fact there are more Hispanic (4.5 percent) than Black (1 percent) residents. But there is a common thread that binds this Southwest Indiana town: basketball. Chuck thinks all this hoop hoopla made him a better baseball player and more promising major league prospect.

The city's passion for the sport still burns like it did in the 1950s and 1960s, a time described as the Hoosier state's heyday of hoops. Terms such as "Sweet Sixteen," "Final Four," and "March Madness" were used in Indiana long before the NCAA and television networks started selling the concept.

In 1925, James Naismith, who invented basketball in Massachusetts, said "basketball really had its origin in Indiana, which remains the center of the sport." He said this after sitting with 15,000 screaming fans at the Indianapolis Exposition Building and then giving out the awards to the champions from Frankfort. Washington High School played before Mr. Naismith in the Final Four. Chuck was a toddler back home, but there was basketball frenzy all around him. In 2010, he would ride in a parade with Naismith's grandson, Ian.

From 1911 to 1997 Indiana had a one-class tournament that ended with only one champion. That meant one loss, and your team was done. For many years, nearly 800 teams were in the contest from every corner of the state; you can imagine the drama and thrill. The tournament helped send Indiana players and coaches, and the sport of basketball, throughout the nation.

Chuck says it helped a lot of Indiana kids, like him, get a college education. "If a college heard you played basketball in Indiana back then, it didn't matter if it was Alaska, they wanted you."

The sensation of such a unique tournament would cause businesses to close and towns to build gyms that were bigger than their population. If you had the biggest field house in the area, you might be awarded one of the sixty-four tourney sites. Although Washington was never that big of a school, the Hatchets were and are a perennial power, and Chuck Harmon played a big role in their success for several years.

Many think Indiana high-school basketball hit its peak in 1990 when Damon Bailey and his Bedford team played before just over 40,000 fans at the Hoosier Dome in Indianapolis. Millions more watched on television. ESPN carried a live feed. Bailey's team was down six late in the game. He scored eleven unanswered points and ran off the court and hugged his grandpa. His legend continued with Bob Knight at IU. Today, he sells truck parts back home in Heltonville, and he still runs camps and signs autographs. It was that kind of atmosphere Chuck and his state champions teammates helped create.

The sport has noticeably waned in recent years, statewide. Most would say it's due to the state athletic association in 1997 changing from the famous and fabulously successful one-class tournament to four different divisions, similar to many other states. It was a controversial decision that many Hoosiers hated. Now, there are multiple champions, but the system is too confusing and diluted for many fans to care about, unless their team is involved. Old habits die hard, and for many self-reliant Hoosiers, just suggesting their kids have to play in a smaller class based upon enrollment riles their feathers. They say it is a feeble attempt at political correctness that rewards titles that weren't earned. Legislating success rather than earning it is very unHoosier-like.

Harmon agrees. But he still loves to see the Hatchets cut down the nets.

In most Indiana communities, and especially Washington, once the ball goes up, there are still plenty of people cheering loudly enough to permanently damage your hearing. Still, most Davids would like a shot at the Goliaths again, with the idea that they would rather lose to the big guy, than knock off somebody their own size. Even though it isn't that big of a school, compared to most in Indiana, Washington has won six state titles, three in the one-class system (1930, 1941, 1942) and three since the tournament expansion (2005, 2008, 2010). The six titles are the third highest of the nearly 1,000 different schools that have participated since the beginning in 1910. Muncie Central has won eight state titles, Marion High School has won seven.

Chuck Harmon is proud of Washington's impressive tradition and unbelievable facilities. The gym he played in still stands. It was built in 1925 and seated 5,200 fans. "Our high-school gym was big compared to most of the teams we faced.... We always had a full house." The "new" arena beside it was completed in time for the 1966–67 season with a couple of thousand more seats.

According to a March 19, 1998, article in the *New York Times*, Indiana has fifteen of the largest sixteen high-school gyms in the United States, if not the world. A *USA Today* article dated February 25, 2004, said that

New Castle, Indiana, has crammed as many as 10,000 people in its high-school basketball cathedral. Washington's Hatchet House would rank about twelfth in the nation as far as prep basketball places go and safely in the top fifteen on the planet. That is pretty impressive for a city with only one McDonalds and a Walmart that's not even super.

It's the coaches, players, and fans who have combined to make Washington something special. Lately, the gym has hosted the top college coaches in the country, thanks to the Zeller family. Currently, six foot ten junior Cody Zeller is wanted by about every top program in the United States. You may not be able to find Washington that easy, but it's a cinch that most big-time coaches and their staffs don't need a GPS. This is not the first rodeo for parents Steve and Lorri Zeller. They have been quite the basketball couple. Cody's seven-foot brother Luke played for Notre Dame and now plays winter ball in Japan and in the Chicago Bulls summer league. His other seven-foot big brother, Tyler, played with the 2009 NCAA champions from the University of North Carolina. He's played well en route to UNC's 2010 NIT runner-up and likely will start for the Tarheels next year.

Name just about any big school, and they want Cody. North Carolina has been to see him three times, and Roy Williams doesn't have the reputation of being on the recruiting road that much. Of course, Indiana's big three IU, Purdue, and Notre Dame, have offers in hand. On the winter night when Chuck went home, Sam Alford was there to check out Tyler. Alford had been a star at Washington, then moved to New Castle to coach. That's where his son Steve broke records and later won a national championship with IU and Bob Knight in 1987. After a successful coaching stint at Iowa, Steve has rebuilt the University of New Mexico program. Word is, he would like young Mr. Zeller to move west. Craig Neal, a former Washington High star, is his assistant coach. He starred for the 1983 Georgia Tech Sweet Sixteen team, then spent four years in the NBA.

The national basketball connections to Chuck's high school seem endless. He's proud to be a part of it.

Chuck moved slowly as he entered a tunnel leading to the area floor on this January night. He was shuffling and used his cane to balance his every step. He wore a Reds baseball cap and a jacket with his name and the number "10" on the back. One of the first people to greet him was Cody Zeller. Chuck is six foot two, but he had to look way up to see the current Washington star. Chuck instantly perked up and immediately began encouraging Cody and his teammate Sam Gines, giving them a little pep talk on what it takes to become a champion. Cody later referred to Chuck as "his buddy." Chuck enjoyed seeing the team all scrubbed and in suits as they watched the reserve game.

He told local sportswriter Mike Myers that he was impressed with the speed and ability of today's players. After one Hatchet player made a quick move from the three-point line to the hoop and scored, Chuck said, "back in our day, you didn't think about doing that."

The movie *Hoosiers* presents a pretty good idea what Washington, Indiana, is like. In Chuck Harmon's glory days, in the early 1940s, the city was considerably bigger than either the fictional town Hickory or Milan, the real-life inspiration for the movie. But a lot was, and is, the same, as what was depicted on the screen, such as the pride-in-work ethic, honesty, religion, and, of course, basketball, basketball, and basketball.

Chuck Harmon's patience and determination would make him the kind of man the Reds could count on to be a special player.

Chuck Harmon was a standout high school basketball player at Washington, Indiana. His teams won two state championships. His Toledo University team made it to the finals of NIT. He was cut by the Boston Celtics of the NBA before focusing on baseball.

The 1941 Washington Hatchets, the Indiana State High School basketball champions. This team finished with a 27-5 record and won the state tournament with 777 teams. First row, left to right: Wininger, Thomas, Riffey, Grove, DonAldson, Chuck Harmon. Second row, left to right: Coach Crawley, Mangin, Crane, J. Dejernett, Bill Harmon, Raney, Manager Boger.

The 1942 Washington Hatchets, the Indiana State High School basketball champions. This team finished with a 30-1 record and won the state tournament with 769 teams. First row, left to right: Chuck Harmon, Raney, Grove, Riffey, Donaldson, J. Dejerrnet. Second row, left to right: Sum, Horrall, Coach Marion Crawley, Crane, Harner.

Jackie Robinson signing the contract offered by Branch Rickey of the Brooklyn Dodgers to become the first African American to play Major League Baseball. Photo courtesy of the Los Angeles Dodgers.

Chuck Harmon was nicknamed "The Glove" because he could play so many positions and had a glove for every assignment.

This is the historic photo of rookie Hank Aaron sliding into third base under Chuck Harmon at Crosley Field in Cincinnati. Aaron broke a bone on this play. Both players were rookies at the time.

During the 1954 and 1955 seasons, Chuck usually led off and played third base. He was known as the fastest player on those Reds teams famous for their home run hitting, with the likes of Ted Kluszewski.

The 1954 Cincinnati Reds. Chuck Harmon is sitting in the second row, sixth from the left. Nino Escalera (top row, far left) was also of African decent. Other outstanding players include Gus Bell (top row, third from left), Joe Nuxhall (top row, fifth from left), Johnny Temple (middle row, second from left), Ted Kluszewski (on Harmon's right), and Wally Post (middle row, third from right).

CINCINNATI REDLEGS—1955

FIFTH PLACE   WON 75   LOST 79

FRONT ROW: J. Temple, H. Landrith, Bat Boy B. Stowe, R. Bridges, R. McMillan, M. Smith, D. Gross, S. Burgess.
SECOND ROW: A. Silvera, A. Fowler, Coach Tom Ferrick, Manager B. Tebbetts, Coach D. Bartell, Coach J. Dykes, B. Podbielan, S. Mele, C. Harmon, J. Collum, Dr. Wayne Anderson, Trainer.
THIRD ROW: J. Murdough, Traveling Secretary; S. Polys, B. Thurman, T. Kluszewski, G. Bell, W. Post, H. Freeman, M. Batts, J. Black, Chesty Evans, Equipment.
BACK ROW: B. Harle, R. Jablonski, R. Minarcin, J. Klippstein, G. Staley, E. Bailey, J. Nuxhall.
Players with Redlegs during part of regular season but not shown: G. Garbus, B. Adams, S. Ridzik, B. Borkowski, A. Seminick, J. Bravia, J. Greengrass, B. Hooper, F. Baczewski, J. Pearce, M. Fisher, J. Lane, C. Valentine, C. Ross, T. Acker.

This is the 1955 Cincinnati Reds. Chuck Harmon is second row, third from the right. Ted Kluszewski hit 47 home runs in 1955. He's standing in the third row, fourth from the left. Joe Nuxhall was the Reds' top pitcher with a 17-12 record and an All-Star game appearance. He is standing in the fourth row, far right.

Chuck Harmon being honored with his own "Day," with his family at Crosley Field in Cincinnati.

Chuck with wife Pearl and daughter Charlene.

Chuck was traded to the St. Louis Cardinals May 16, 1956 for Alex Grammas and Joe Frazier. Before Chuck left the Reds, he helped the second African American for the ball club, Frank Robinson, who would become one of the greatest ever to play the game. Robinson would be an MVP in both leagues and the first African American manager in both leagues.

Chuck Harmon would be the second African American to play for the Philadelphia Phillies, following John Kennedy in 1957.

This is Chuck with the great Jesse Owens. Owens achieved international fame by winning four gold medals in the 1936 summer olympics in Berlin, Germany. Adolf Hitler was using the games to prove German superiority. Despite Hitler's annoyance, owens was cheered enthusiastically by 110,000 people in Berlin's Olympic Stadium. Similar to Chuck's experience, Owens was most often not allowed to stay in the same hotels as white athletes.

Chuck, Pearl, and a friend visit with one of baseball's all-time greats, Willie Mays. Willie and Chuck competed head to head for several seasons.

Leroy Robert (Satchel) Paige with Cincinnati's Charlie "Whip" Davis. Both played in the Negro Leagues. Satchel is the most famous Negro League player and was the oldest rookie to play Major League Baseball At the age of 42. He was still playing professional baseball until he was around 60. Nobody ever really knew how old Satchel was.

Oscar Robertson and Chuck in 2010 At a parade in downtown Indianapolis, where both were honored for being among Indiana's great basketball players of all time. "The Big O" was one of the greatest players ever at the University of Cincinnati and in the NBA. He is the only player in NBA history to average a triple-double for an entire season. Oscar suffered from racism when his Crispus Attucks high school team won back-to-back state championships, a first-ever for an all-black school in Indiana.

Photo By Marty Pieratt

This is Chuck's family in later years. From left: Savanna, Ruth Lois, Sherman, Bill, Millicent, Josephine, Jean, and Farrell. Missing from the photo are Chuck, Rose, and Joyce. Chuck's mom, Rosa, died in 1959; his dad Sherman passed in 1974.

Pearl joins Chuck as he is inducted into the Indiana High School Baseball Hall of Fame. He's also in the Basketball Hall of Fame.

Chuck's sister-in-law, Thelma, and nephews Bill (on left) and Tom. Chuck's late brother William founded Harmon Construction Company and Harmon Steel Corporation. It is now one of the largest minority-owned corporations in the United States, based in North Vernon, Indiana. Bill played basketball at the University of Louisville and made it to the Final Four with coach Denny Crum. Tom played baseball at Indiana University.

Chuck Harmon gathers with family and friends at Great American Ball Park for the dedication of his plaque. To the right side of the plaque is Chuck Harmon Jr. Kneeling before him is Chuck's daughter, Cheryl. The plaque now is outside the stadium wall near the front entrance. It reads: On April 17th 1954, seven years after Jackie Robinson broke baseball's color barrier, Charles Byron (Chuck) Harmon made his Major League debut as the first African American to play for the Cincinnati Reds. Harmon spent four seasons in the majors with the Reds, Cardinals, and Phillies before hanging up his spikes in 1957. He has streets and Little League fields named in his honor and he has received countless civic and humanitarian awards, including the Martin Luther King Jr. award in 1996. Chuck still calls Cincinnati his home and remains one of the most prominent and beloved citizens of the city.

Chuck with Barry Larkin, one of Cincinnati's all-time favorite players.

Chuck joins Reds manager Dusty Baker for a few laughs. Baker had an outstanding playing career with Atlanta, Los Angeles, San Francisco, and Oakland. Along with the Reds, he has managed the Giants and Cubs.

Chuck and Hank Aaron swapping some old stories. Aaron was the last Negro League player to play in Major League Baseball. He surpassed Babe Ruth as the Home Run King. He finished his career with 755 home runs. When he was just 18, he led the Indianapolis Clowns to a 1952 Negro League World Series title.

Ken Griffey, Jr. And Adam Dunn hanging out with Chuck before a Reds game a few years back at Great American Ball Park.

Cincinnati Bengals coach Marvin Lewis and chief executive officer of the Cincinnati Reds Robert Castellini, talking baseball and football with Chuck.

Chuck greeting Muhammed Ali before the 2009 Major League Baseball Civil Rights Game.

Comedian Bill Cosby shakes hands with Chuck; Chuck's brother Sherman was a good friend of Cosby's brother in Philadelphia. They both volunteered at the YMCA.

The first two African Americans to play for the Cincinnati Reds, Chuck
Harmon and Frank Robinson. Robinson credits chuck with helping launch his
career. Robinson was the first Black MVP in both leagues and first manager
in both leagues. They played together for Cincinnati in 1956.

Chuck with Hall of Famer Tommy John and Charlie "Whip" Davis. Like Chuck, John was an Indiana high school basketball and baseball star. John played at Terre Haute Gerstmeyer High School. John won 288 games as a Major League pitcher. He played most of his career for the Dodgers, but also played for the Yankees, Indians, White Sox, Angels, and Athletics. Today he may be best known for a revolutionary arm ligament procedure, now known as the Tommy John surgery. Today it's common for pitchers to have Tommy John surgery during their careers. John said he decided to retire when Mark McGwire got two hits off of him in 1989. McGwire's father was John's dentist. "When your dentist's kid starts hitting you, it's time to retire." Davis played for the Memphis Red Sox of the Negro American League. He was nicknamed "Whip" by his roommate Charlie Pride, who later gave up baseball and became a country singer. Davis owned and operated an auto repair shop in Cincinnati after his baseball career.

Chuck does a little celebrating in front of Hinkle Fieldhouse the day after his high school team from Washington, Indiana, won its sixth championship. This is also the morning after Butler University played its way to the 2010 Final Four. Butler plays its home games here. This is also where Chuck won his state championships in 1941 and 1942. The high school championship round is now played in downtown Indianpolis at Conseco Fieldhouse. The 2010 NCAA Championships were played downtown at Lucas Oil Stadium.

Photo By Marty Pieratt

Seven-foot high school star Cody Zeller and teammate Sam Gines, visit with Chuck at the Hatchet House in Washington, Indiana. Zeller, like his brothers before him (Luke and Tyler), is one of the most sought-after high school players in the nation. All three brothers won state championships at Washington. Luke played for Notre Dame; Tyler plays for North Carolina.

Photo By Marty Pieratt

Chuck Harmon is honored before a crowd of nearly 7,000 prior to a high school game in early 2010 at his hometown of Washington, Indiana.

Photo By Marty Pieratt

104

This is really where it all started for Chuck. This was the Washington High School gym from 1925 until 1966. It serves as the junior high gym today. It was built to hold 5,200 fans. John Wooden, the hall of fame coach at UCLA, played in the first game ever held on this court, on November 26, 1925. His Martinsville team defeated Washington 47-33. It was a rare occasion for Chuck's team to ever lose here. On this Saturday morning in January of 2010, Chuck showed the youngsters he still had his touch.

Photo By Marty Pieratt

Sunday, March 28, 2010, Chuck relaxes at The Columbia Club in downtown Indianapolis. Beside him is official White House china used by Abraham Lincoln during his presidency. Lincoln grew up in Indiana not far from Chuck's hometown of Washington. Lincoln is known for preserving the Union during the Civil War and ending slavery. Chuck's great-great grandfather, Emory Allen, was in the first all-black Civil War regiment. He was killed on November 30, 1864, as he fought for freedom on a battle field in Honey Hill, South Carolina. He had taken a train from Indianapolis to Reidsville, Massachusetts, to volunteer. He was survived by his wife Eliza and seven children.   *Photo By Marty Pieratt*

Race and Rights

Chuck Harmon's ancestry is quite clear. He comes from a group of highly determined people. His great-great-grandfather took a train to Massachusetts so he could join the first all-Black regiment of the Civil War. Emory Allen was killed on the battlefield at Honey Hill, South Carolina, on November 30, 1864.

Chuck's heritage begins in slavery. On his dad's side of the family, Jacob Hawkins (1792–1864) was a slave who escaped to Indiana. There, he aided many slaves as they fled to freedom. Chuck's dad, Sherman, was an educated man. He was one of the first African Americans to attend college at what is now Indiana State University. He would teach at Black schools and work for the B&O railroad. Chuck's mom's family is from Virginia. It was Rosa's great-grandfather who fought in the Civil War after living free in Indianapolis. Eventually members of the family would move south to Washington. That's where Sherman Harmon and Rosa Lawhorn would meet, marry, and build a family with twelve kids.

Thelma Harmon, who married Chuck's older brother Bill, remembers what it was like with so many family and friends. Just getting enough food was a challenge. "I know he [Sherman] always had two big gardens, and she [Rosa] would can everything she could get her hands on."

However, to really understand the history of the Harmons, you have to study the culture of Washington, Indiana. Just before, during, and after the Civil War, it was known as a place that was friendly to African Americans. Washington newspaperman Mike Myers says that has always been an acknowledged fact. "I don't know, it just always has been, as long as I can remember. There have just always been Black families around. It's true over around [nearby] Princeton in Gibson County, too. There are a lot of Black farmers there."

Plenty of Indiana communities have prided themselves on being lily-White, but Washington isn't one of them. That's not to say the town hasn't been without its incidents or problems, but there was much more mutual respect between Whites and Blacks in Washington, Indiana, than in most places in the United States. A key reason may be the success and respect gained by African Americans who believed in the American dream even before the Constitution supported those dreams.

According to Bob Padgett and other local historians, former slaves were two of the earliest inhabitants of Washington and Daviess County. Jake Hawkins came in 1806, and Issac Ballow came a few years later. The Hawkins family would have eleven children and an impressive estate of more than 1,000 acres. The family also prospered by selling land to the railroads and by mining. They were big supporters of Republicans, "the party of Lincoln." They helped establish Black schools, churches, and businesses.

Initially, most southern Indiana pioneers weren't adamantly anti-slavery. Most of the early inhabitants of Indiana came from slave states and likely saw slaves as property. But that changed over time as people witnessed firsthand slaves risking their lives and leaving their families for the freedom that awaited them in the Indiana or Ohio territories. That's why so many anti-slavery Quakers started coming from Ohio, like President Richard Nixon's family in Jennings County, helping to establish the Underground Railroad in Indiana. Christian churches—particularly the Churches of Christ (still prominent in Southern Indiana, Ohio, and Kentucky), under the leadership of Alexander Campbell—had a very strong aversion to slavery.

Southern Indiana's residents also turned against slavery when they witnessed Blacks being kidnapped and taken back to the South, even when they'd been born free in Indiana. Anti-slavery leagues were formed all along the state's southern tier to ensure there were boats and skiffs to aid people trying to escape. Once people were picked up along the "railroad," they were sheltered and fed at "stations," homes and businesses along the way to freedom. Cincinnati, Chicago, and Canada were the primary destinations.

There were two Underground Railroad routes near Chuck's birthplace. His hometown was said to be "a short distance above the mouth of the Little Pigeon." From this crossing the route went through Warrick County then north to Daviess and Greene counties, and finally north to Lake Michigan.

More slaves likely crossed around Jeffersonville, Indiana, and around Louisville than anywhere. Several secret routes included the help and cooperation of brave citizens in Jennings, Jefferson, Jackson, Decatur, Rush, and Fayette counties. If slaves could reach the Quaker community of Richmond, the future was much brighter. Then they were piloted across southwest Ohio to Lake Erie and then into Canada. (Letters, newspaper articles, and reports about the Underground Railroad are available at www.undergroundrailroadindiana.com.)

This was the spirit that surrounded the Harmons as they and other African Americans established their families in Washington, Indiana. But there were other reasons why Daviess County became home to so many Black families. Three included the building of the railroads, the Civil War, and eventually, basketball, which helped overcome the KKK's resistance to democracy.

Railroads

In the first decade of the twentieth century, many Hispanics moved to southern Indiana because they could find work and freedom. The story was much the same for Blacks fleeing the South before, during, and after the Civil War. Nowadays, people are seeking manufacturing jobs in places like Seymour; then, the draw was the railroads in towns like Washington.

Cincinnati was a prosperous place on the Ohio River around 1830, particularly when compared to a swampy place in the middle of the Hoosier state called Indianapolis. Thanks in part to the railroads, the village of Indianapolis eventually would become a super bowl city. Today, it is one of the largest cities in the world not situated beside a major body of water.

One of the first rail lines in America climbed north out of the southern Indiana city of Madison toward Indianapolis in 1838. Just before the Civil War, Indiana began to forsake a transportation system of canals for rail lines. In the decades after the war, Indiana was truly the crossroads of America with famous rail lines and trains, such as the Wabash Cannonball. By 1870, Indianapolis was the stopping point for over 100 trains a day, according to the Indiana State Historical Society at indianahistory.org. If there is one thing that Washington, Indiana, is known for—other than basketball—it is railroads; during its rail heyday, 100 or more trains a day would visit it as well. The Ohio & Mississippi Railroad was laid across southern Indiana from Cincinnati to St. Louis around 1857. Baltimore & Ohio Southwestern (later B&O) took over in 1893.

Washington is just about the perfect middle point between St. Louis and Cincinnati. That's why there are a lot of Reds and Cardinal fans there, and that's why the B&O invested a lot of money into the community. Trains have been rambling through the city since the 1850s; around 1880, B&O installed a huge roundhouse and a railroad car-rebuilding center on sixty acres.

The Civil War

Indiana was, without question, a Union state in the Civil War. It was one of the first to respond to President Abraham Lincoln's initial call for 75,000 troops to take on the Confederacy. Before the war was over, 208,367 Hoosier men responded to defeat the South, perhaps more than from any other state. Chuck's hometown and the surrounding county were proud to take part. By the time the conflict ended in 1865, 24,416 Indiana men had died during service. It's estimated that more than 50,000 others returned home with serious wounds or scars.

The war was fought to preserve the Union and end the battle over slavery. Because Indiana gave so much to the effort, it's understandable that places like Washington practiced what they had preached and remembered why they had sacrificed. Today on the courthouse square is a huge monument to Daviess County's effort to preserve the Union and "free all men." The county lost 2,312 men in the Civil War.

Initially, even Indiana was against sending Black troops to fight for the cause, but as the war raged on and casualties mounted, African Americans were asked and gladly joined the fight. It likely meant the freedom of many friends and relatives back in the South.

Massachusetts was the first state to recruit Black soldiers. In fact, agents from the 54th Massachusetts Regiment came to Indiana to find African American soldiers. This may have been why Chuck's great-great grandfather, Emory Allen, took the train to join up at Reidsville, Massachusetts. He was already forty and had five kids, but the opportunity to fight for freedom was too important.

That regiment was depicted in the movie *Glory*. Blacks from all the states and Canada served in it, including Frederick Douglas's son and Emory Allen.

By late 1863, Indiana had its own Black regiment, the 28th United States Colored Troops (USCT). Troops came from throughout Indiana and a few recently emancipated slaves from across the river in Kentucky, with names like Brawdy, McCowen, Shafer, and Evans. They headed straight for battle, and half were killed or wounded fighting for freedom that arguable wouldn't be seen for nearly 100 years. (Indiana-focused Civil War information is available through Craig Dunn Civil War books and compilations and online at www.civilwarindiana.com.)

The KKK

Not long ago, a member of the Harmon family laughed when he remembered at story from one of the old-timers in the family. It was said that the Harmons thought it was a good idea to keep a White sheet hidden in the trunk of the car just in case you happened upon an "unfriendly rally." While the idea of Black person covered with a sheet, fooling the fools, may sound a bit humorous, there were scary moments for the Harmons and other Black people in southern Indiana.

The state that brought us the likes of Tavis Smiley, Michael Jackson, and Oscar Robertson also gave us D. C. Stephenson, a Texas man who moved to Chuck's region of the state to help form the Ku Klux Klan. He nearly took his White robe and cross-burning ways to the Indiana governor's mansion, and his efforts helped spread the Klan's disease from the South to the Midwest and beyond, according to the *Encyclopedia of Indianapolis* and other references, including *The Dragon and the Cross: The Rise and Fall of the Ku Klux Klan in Middle America* by Richard K. Tucker.

In the 1920s nearly 30 percent of American-born Caucasian men in Indiana had ties to the KKK, according to documents and studies produced by the Indiana Historical Society and Leonard Moore at the University of California. Much of the organization was formed just a few dozen miles away from what Chuck always remembers as his "happy home."

The Klan first appeared in the South following the Civil War. Most historians agree it originated with six men in Pulaski, Tennessee. What seemed to start as a harmless quasi-fraternal organization was transformed by the appearance of vigilantes looking for violence. Confederate General Nathan Bedford Forrest was chosen to be the first leader of the group, which was determined to put Blacks "back in their place" and to chase White scoundrels and carpetbaggers back to the North. Death and violence soon followed wherever this group would ride.

At one point, the Klan nearly died out, but it lingered and finally came back to strength as the nation was gearing up for World War I, around 1915. The KKK sold its membership on the need to defend America against not only Blacks but also Germans, Jews, Catholics, Socialists, and even union leaders.

Klansmen in the South recruited Stephenson to organize in Indiana. He started his hateful and racist work around Evansville. His full-time job was selling bonds for a coal company, but his other job was selling White supremacy. Stephenson asked early Indiana recruits if they were native born, White, gentile American citizens and if they would "faithfully strive for the eternal maintenance of White Supremacy."

With peer pressure and his speaking charisma, Stephenson's organization grew in size and political power. If you wanted to get ahead in Indiana politics in the early 1920s, the KKK could be the bridge to success. He was often quoted as saying, "I am the law in Indiana." He convinced churches and legitimate fraternal organizations that the Klan was an important warrior in the fight against "moral decay."

Chuck Harmon was born about an hour from where Stephenson was doing his dirty work. Washington was the scene of KKK marches when Chuck was three or four years old. These were "frightened men who hit their faces behind masks and attempted to intimidate churches and other town associations," according to local historians Bob Padgett, Keith Ellis, and Martha DeJernett House. They claim that in the 1920s a Washington mineworker was killed due to Klan-related activity. But the KKK's ignorance and failure was exposed in Washington because of the community's long-help belief in community pride and brotherhood.

It all came crashing down on Indiana's Klan king, Stephenson, when he was arrested and charged with the murder of statehouse secretary Madge Oberholtzer. He reportedly held her against her will, attacking and raping her in his private railcar. She took poison in an apparent effort to be released by him and died a month later. Reports suggest there was never an official ruling on why she died: the poison or the human bites on her body.

Stephenson likely was confident of getting a pardon from Governor Ed Jackson, whom he had helped elect. When his old political cronies didn't help him get out of prison, he started singing, most notably to the *Indianapolis Times*. The paper won a Pulitzer Prize for its stories on Stephenson, the Klan, and dirty politicians. Many resigned from office or were sent to jail for accepting KKK bribes.

Those who fought the Klan's involvement in Chuck's community could now rest a bit easier.

Stephenson spent thirty-one years in prison before being released in 1956. The Klan faded to a seemingly powerless, cult status in the Hoosier state, but is alive in select caves and crevices in Indiana and across the nation, where the spirit of hate and its putrid smell still lingers.

Dave DeJernett

Sports have always had a way of bringing Americans together. It happened with Jackie Robinson in 1947 and Chuck Harmon in 1954. It happened around Chuck's hometown in 1930. Chuck may have been the man who crossed the racial divide in the name of sports in Cincinnati, but in his hometown, it was Dave DeJernett.

In the spring of 1913, the B&O Railroad asked John DeJernett to move his wife, Mary, and baby son, Dave, to Washington. His help was needed to rebuild a trestle that had collapsed with a steam engine killing four workers. For twelve cents an hour, they made the move. Dave was about ten years older than Chuck and grew up a few blocks from the Harmon house in Washington's West End. DeJernett's impact upon the White and Black citizens of the community would be unmatched.

Like Chuck did a few years later, Dave attended an all-Black elementary school known as Dunbar. Washington High School hired a basketball-crazy coach in Burl Friddle. He had been a three-time state champion at Franklin High School, and the team stayed together in that city to become national champions in 1923 at Franklin College. Chuck Harmon remembers Coach Friddle and that a lady named Lena Dunn helped him build a basketball program before most people in America knew what a basketball was. When Friddle was looking for basketball players, he didn't see color. When he was asked to help with the physical education of the Black kids at Dunbar, he discovered Dave, kind, good-natured, and a lover of farm work and basketball.

Dave DeJernett was not the first African American to play Washington basketball; that was Dave and Harold Bledsoe back around 1914, the same year Joe Umbles and Richard Ballou won state track titles. But Dave was the first local superstar.

Coach Friddle used the tall, athletic DeJernett in the middle, and he may have been the first in the country to use a center, pivot-player much the way the position is used today. In 1930, Dave led the Hatchets to their first state championship with a 32 to 31 win over Muncie Central. The Hatchets were the only team standing of the 760 that had started playing about a month earlier. Dave was the first Black athlete in U.S. history to star on an undisputed, integrated, statewide or national championship basketball team. According to the historian Padgett, two other teams in Chicago and New York won titles but not in state or national competition.

DeJernett came within a couple of points of doing it again in 1931 as the team made the Final Four out of 766 teams that began play. He went on to star at Indiana Central (now University of Indianapolis), going 16–1 and regarded as one of the best teams in the nation. He competed against and became friends with Ray Crowe, who was Oscar Robertson's high-school coach. Robertson's brother Bailey went to DeJernett's college and from there to the Harlem Globetrotters.

DeJernett encouraged Black kids across the country. Back at home, his success cemented relationships among Blacks and Whites in the community and created a more positive environment for Chuck Harmon.

"You know, really, it was a great place to grow up," Chuck says.

Two-Time Champions

The 1940–41 Championship Season

MUCH OF THE WORLD WAS ENGAGED IN a war, and the United States government was giving serious thought to joining the fight. Hitler was on a rampage, invading countries and breaking treaties. President Franklin Delano Roosevelt didn't know that Japan was planning an attack upon Pearl Harbor, but it was obvious that trouble was brewing.

All across the United States there was continuous chatter about war and the potential draft, but back in Washington, Indiana, basketball was the preferred topic at the barbershop and local diner. The Hatchets were going to be powerful, with the likes of Leroy "Hook" Mangin and the two Harmon brothers, Chuck and Bill. Others on the team were Jim Riffey, Art Grove, John DeJernett, Ivan Wininger, Bob Donaldson, Garland Raney, Forrest Crane, Calvin Thomas, and Don Dougherty.

The club was coming off a 25–5 season and had it not been for Mitchell High School, they may have won it all. They lost the five games by a total of fifteen points and were unbeaten at home. A young man by the name of Rufus Arnold destroyed opponents. He got a lot of help from Mangin, who ended up playing at IU. They were so good that their freshmen, including Chuck Harmon, played against other varsity teams and won most of those games.

Marion Crawley, who won four state titles before he hung up his clipboard, coached the Hatchets.

The chant "Wash-ing-ton in forty-one" would be relished by the locals and hated by their foes. Chuck was just having fun. He loved to play ball.

As the Battle of Britain raged, the Washington community cheered their team, which was competing against teams from Petersburg, Bloomfield, and a strong Bedford team. Washington was on a role that would not stop until March, although there were speed bumps along the way. The Hatchets suffered their first defeat of the season against their arch-rival and conference foe Vincennes, 24 to 15. As disappointing as the defeat must have been to many people in the Washington community, they also were worried about the ramifications of the war in Europe. The bombing raids of London and Manchester were just beginning, and the future of Europe began to look very bleak. In the next game Washington failed to rebound against a strong Jeffersonville team in a tight 34 to 33 game. Then Washington enjoyed three straight wins over Jeffersonville, conference rival Jasper, and Laporte.

The next step was a trip to Vincennes, for what was called the Big Four Tournament. Rivals Vincennes, Jasper, Huntingburg, and Washington were the teams involved. Washington very narrowly defeated Huntingburg 33 to 32 in a very hard-fought game. The Hatchets could not escape Jasper's high-powered attack, however, and were defeated by the score of 45 to 34.

Coach Crowley said the team was starting to gel. The Hatchets went on a ten-game winning streak. The *Washington Times-Herald* called Chuck "slinky" and said he "was learning great under-basket timing and a fingertip touch on the ball."

The war in Europe started to rage in Africa. Erwin Rommel was appointed head of the newly created German unit Africa Corps to attack British strategic locations.

The Hatchets piled up many wins and miles on the team bus. They knocked off rival Vincennes, and then took Jasper in an overtime thriller. Chuck came up huge in the overtime game with ten points. He also controlled the court in wins over Vincennes and Fort Wayne Central.

Washington's winning streak ended with a 33 to 32 defeat at Greencastle. But in the final regular season game of the 1940–41 season, the Washington Hatchets defeated Bloomington, 38 to 27.

Despite the raging war, Indiana turned its eyes toward basketball. For at least a few weeks, Hoosier hysteria became the news. The Hatchets' post-season journey to the state championship began at home. In the first round, Washington failed to be a gracious host by eliminating Odon, 60 to 16. Washington continued its sectional run by defeating Plainville, 52 to 35, with Harmon leading the scoring with thirteen points. The Hatchets then defeated a Shoals team by eight points. The Washington Hatchets were only one win away from lifting the sectional trophy in front of a home crowd. Harmon responded to the pressure by leading the scoring with seventeen against Loogootee in a 48 to 36 win.

While Washington was preparing for its regional games, anti-Nazi protests began all across the United States. The common sentiment across the country had turned against the Germans. Even with the political turmoil, basketball still continued to be played in Indiana. In the Washington regional, Washington defeated Shelburn, 52 to 34, carried by Harmon's sixteen points. Washington defeated Freelandville in the regional finals, 54 to 43.

Two rounds down, two to go for glory. It was off to the Sweet 16. Washington won the state semi-state by beating Evansville Bosse and Bedford, 44 to 27 and 44 to 32. It was Final Four time at Historic Hinkle Fieldhouse.

On March 22, 1941, two days before Rommel began his first offensive in Africa, the state title games were held at Butler Fieldhouse. Washington won its second state title by defeating Kokomo, 48 to 32, with an eight-point effort from Harmon, and Madison, 39 to 33. Chuck picked up nine in that one. He was named to the *Indianapolis News* all-State first team for 1941. The final statistics for Harmon in 1940–41 were thirty-two games played, 263 total points, and an average of 8.2 points scored per game.

The celebration in Indianapolis headed back home to Washington. Out of 777 teams that began this one tournament, Washington was the champion. One of the hottest tickets in town was the victory dinner at St. Mary's auditorium. With so many stars like Chuck Harmon returning, it didn't take long for folks to start thinking about a repeat.

The 1941–42 Championship Season

If things were tense in the days preceding the bombing of Pearl Harbor, they reached a crisis level in the days following the attack on December 7, 1941. Two thousand, four hundred and two lost their lives and 1,282 were wounded in the attack by the Japanese.

In Washington, it meant several thousand young men and some women would be leaving the safety of this small Indiana town to fight oversees in the Asian and European theaters. However, for the folks at home, praying for safety and hope for a soldiers' letter were of more concern than was Hatchet basketball. Still, the sport was the perfect escape for a war-weary community who followed the war by listening to the radio and reading Hoosier Ernie Pyle's newspaper stories from the battle lines.

Getting to the top is extremely difficult. Staying there is nearly impossible. But that's exactly what Chuck Harmon and his teammates set out to do in late fall of 1941. Even though 769 teams would enter the tournament, Chuck Harmon and his teammates were quite certain they could do it again.

Brother Bill had graduated, but Chuck was joined by talented Art Grove, who would later play with him on the University of Toledo's NIT championship team. Also on this solid team were James Riffey, John DeJernett, Garland Raney, Bob Donaldson, Mere Horrall, Norman Harner, Forrest Crane, Bob Sum, and Robert Fletcher.

If Washington's 1940–41 championship team was impressive, the 1941–42 club was legendary. Chuck's team was ranked number one off the bat and won by an average of 14.6 points per game. The key to the Washington team was its defense, which allowed only 24.2 points per game, an unthinkable number by today's standards and an extremely impressive feat at the time. The team also finished 11–1 in their conference play with a one-point loss to Evansville Central. That's the same school where Lee Hamilton would star a few years later, taking his team to the championship game. Today, Hamilton is known for his many years in U.S. Congress, his foreign affairs expertise and negotiating ability, and for chairing the 9/11 Commission and the Iraq Study Group.

Only a couple of months before the attack on Pearl Harbor, the Washington Hatchets began their historic 1941–42 season by defeating Petersburg, 46 to 31. Washington continued its dominance by defeating Bedford and conference rival Jasper in front of a crowd of 4,000 fans in dramatic fashion. Led by Chuck, the Hatchets went on a 12 to 5 run to win the game. The Hatchets continued to display fourth-quarter dominance by outscoring the Vincennes Alices 15 to 4 in the final quarter to win 37 to 21.

Playing the toughest teams sometimes hours away, Washington continued to win in dominant fashion, defeating Muncie Central, Bicknell, Jeffersonville, Franklin, and Delphi by an average of twenty points a game. Washington entered the Big Four Tournament with a record of 9–0. The Hatchets lived up to expectations by defeating Vincennes, 34 to 26, in the opener and defeating Huntingburg, 34 to 27, in the championship game. Chuck and his teammates looked unstoppable.

After the December 7, 1941, attack on Pearl Harbor, the United States jumped into World War II in both the Asian and Pacific theaters. There was a determined mood across the country to retaliate and get the job done. Sometimes the crowds at Indiana basketball games reflected the urgency of wartime middle America. It seemed that each family had somebody in uniform risking their life.

The season rolled on for high-school kids like Chuck, who knew the real world was just a few months away. The news wasn't good. The events overseas did not look positive. The Japanese imperial army captured Wake Island and defeated the British and Canadian armies in Hong Kong.

Meanwhile, on the court, Washington continued its winning streak with impressive and dominating wins over Mitchell, Jasper, and Evansville Reitz. The 15–0 Hatchets moved to 15–1 with the team's first (and only) loss to Evansville Central. It was an extremely tight one-point game in front of the largest crowd to ever witness a high-school basketball game in Evansville. Washington trailed 31 to 24 in the final quarter but managed to close in within one point on a Harmon free throw. The Hatchets almost won on a last chance shot by Harmon and fellow teammate John DeJernett, but both attempts failed to get in the basket. The Hatchets lost 32 to 31.

More bad news continued to come from overseas; the siege of Bataan began in the Philippines. In only a few months, the Philippines would be lost, and many Americans would be killed in the fighting.

Washington continued to ignore the distractions by defeating New Albany by nineteen points. Harmon led the Hatchets with seventeen points to defeat Vincennes, 36 to 23. The team then closed out the regular season by victories over Huntingburg, Martinsville, Greencastle, and Bloomington.

The 769-team tournament began at sixty-four sectional tournament sites. Chuck and his number one–ranked club had the advantage of being one of the hosts. If you won the sectional, you were one of sixty-four teams playing at sixteen sites. Victory there meant you were part of the "Sweet Sixteen" playing at four sites, which produced the Final Four.

Washington impressed hometown fans by winning their first round sectional game over Loogootee, 57 to 23. Washington went on to defeat Montgomery by twenty points in the second round of the sectional. The Hatchets were gracious hosts to absolutely no one. They won the sectional championship by destroying Elnora, 55 to 17. The Hatchets opened the Washington Regional by defeating Sullivan, 53–29, and slipped by Jasper by three on the backs on Jim Riffey and Harmon's combined twenty-two points.

Now they were in the final sixteen. Chuck later thanked the reserves he battled in practice. "Leo Klier and Rufus Arnold really made us the ballplayers we were. In practice, we had bruises all over us." At the semi-state, Washington avenged its loss to Evansville Central and rode to the Final Four by beating Bedford in the final game, 37 to 20. On March 21, 1942—only a few months before the turning point of the war in the Pacific, the Battle of Midway—Washington became the fourth team to win consecutive state titles at Hinkle Fieldhouse. The Hatchets defeated Frankfort, 42 to 32, in the afternoon game with a solid nine points from Harmon. In the final high-school game of Chuck's career, he and the Hatchets took out Muncie Burris in a defensive, slow-down bout, 24 to 18. Garland Raney had the go-ahead points to break a tie. They had done it again.

For a few hours anyway, moms and dads, sisters and brothers, would relish their accomplishment before going back to thoughts of war and hopes of peace.

In 1942, Chuck Harmon received the honor of being named an Indiana All-Star, and he played against Kentucky's best that summer. He remembers a Kentuckian "who looked like Colonel Sanders" running up to greet him because of how well he and the Indiana team played. "He said he usually didn't speak to people like me [i.e., Black], but he just had to shake my hand." Maybe Chuck was bringing people together even then.

The honors for Chuck have continued in Indiana for over fifty years. He was named to the silver anniversary basketball team in 1967 and inducted into the Indiana Basketball Hall of Fame in 1989. During the 1941–42 season, he played in thirty-one total games, scored a total of 261 points and averaged 8.4 points per game. There would be many days of celebrating and relishing the victory back home in Washington. But before long it was time to think of college, that is, if he didn't have to go to war right away. Chuck had the grades and the athletic ability to be a college student-athlete, but would he have the opportunity?

Tenacious in Toledo

There were a lot of places closer to home where Chuck would have loved to play college basketball, but he ended up packing a small bag and going to the University of Toledo in Ohio. A few months later Chuck and the Rockets would play against St. John's University for the national championship before a packed crowd at New York's Madison Square Garden. Was it intimidating for an Indiana country kid to play before 18,233 people?

"No," says Chuck. "I had played before crowds almost that size in high school back in Indiana. That wasn't a problem." As for why he went to the University of Toledo, well, it was big enough school where Chuck could get a good education, play basketball and baseball, and a strong local connection—you might say a Hoosier hoops pipeline. His first choice would have been Indiana University up the road in Bloomington, but this was five years before IU would break the Big Ten color barrier in basketball by offering Jim Garrett a scholarship. IU had done it in football, but no school in the league had Black basketball players yet.

But Coach Burl Friddle convinced Chuck that Toledo was a great place to play both basketball and baseball. His team was coming off a final four appearance in the NIT. If that names rings a bell in this story, it should: Friddle was the coach at Washington High School when the team won it all in 1930. Chuck had been in grade school, but he remembered Friddle; more important, Friddle knew where he could get players who could take a team all the way. Friddle took Harmon and Art Grove from southern Indiana to the Big Apple before St. John's ended their hopes of following up a state title with a national trophy. Also on the team were Bob Bolyard and Dallas Zuber from Ft. Wayne. Friddle had coached there, too.

Toledo made it to the final game with wins over Manhattan (54 to 47) and Washington & Jefferson (46 to 39). St. John's beat Rice (51 to 49) and Fordham (60 to 58). "The NIT was the big tournament back then," Chuck remembers. "St. John's beat us, but it was a close game most of the way. At halftime, we were down 22 to 16, and then they went on a spree. At that time you could goal tend, and they had a big center, about seven foot." His name was Harry J. "Big Boy" Boykoff. He blocked so many shots he is said to be the key reason goal tending was ruled illegal. The center from Brooklyn once scored 54 for St. John's; later, as a Boston Celtic, he was the highest paid player in the NBA at the time. After his basketball career ended, his size helped him get parts on television shows, such as *Star Trek*. But Chuck just remembers as Boykoff as the "alien" who killed Toledo's chances of a 1943 NIT Title.

Twenty-five of Toledo's twenty-seven points came from those four Indiana boys, but St. John's won 48 to 27. Chuck had six points.

Because of the war, Toledo didn't play basketball again until the 1946–47 season. Chuck, like many others, was called to war. After three years in the navy, he came back to the university. Although records and statistics are fuzzy and unavailable from the University of Toledo, Chuck seems to have played on teams that were a combined 74–27 for a remarkable winning percentage of .733. These teams reportedly won by record margins of fifty-four against Cedarville and fifty-three against Defiance. They lost a close game to the eventual NCAA champion Holy Cross, led by future Celtic player and Hall-of-Famer Bob Cousy, 42 to 39.

Coach Friddle was wired for success in basketball. He won a 1920 state championship as a player for Indiana's Franklin High School and was captain of the undefeated national champions at Franklin College (1922). There is a banner in their arena today honoring Friddle and the "Wonder Five."

On the baseball side, Chuck would be one of ten Toledo Rocket players to make it to Major League Baseball, including Stan Clarke, Scott Fletcher, Mitch Maier, Tom Marsh, Bob Meyer, Denny Stark, Marc Wilkins, A.J. Sager, and Len Matuszek. Like Chuck, Matuszek played both basketball and baseball for the University of Toledo. He is possibly most famous for taking Pete Rose's job as the first baseman for the Philadelphia Phillies. Tommy Lasorda and the Los Angeles Dodgers dumped him after he was injured. He tired his hand at WLWT, the television station in Cincinnati, after his playing days. One of his first assignments was to cover Damon Bailey from Bedford, Indiana, who later was named the high-school player of the year and Bob Knight said that, even as an eighth-grader, he could start in college.

The War

Chuck's great-great grandfather, Emory Allen, fought and died in the Civil War. Yet eighty years later, Chuck really didn't have the same opportunity to fight for his country. The navy seemed to want him more for playing baseball than for fighting the Japanese or Germans.

In the Navy

Cʜᴜᴄᴋ Hᴀʀᴍᴏɴ ɪs ᴀs ᴘᴀᴛʀɪᴏᴛɪᴄ ᴀ ꜰᴇʟʟᴏᴡ as you will find. Even though he was having a stellar freshman basketball season at the University of Toledo, he was ready to serve when he was drafted in April 1943. He had barely hung up his basketball shoes after playing for the NIT title at Madison Square Garden. Uncle Sam came calling, and Chuck packed his bags again.

"When your number came, you went," he remembers. "I was stationed at Great Lakes [Illinois] at the Naval Center." Chuck would be there for most of the three years he was in the navy. He would stay until just after the war ended in 1945. By the spring of 1946, he would be back at school. He was one of approximately 167,000 Blacks who served in the navy during the war, or about 4 percent, according to official Department of the Navy statistics.

Looking back, World War II was the first time Blacks were allowed to have anything close to acceptable participation in fighting for their country. "At the war's end, a greater variety of experience existed than had ever before been available within the American Military Establishment," writes Army historian Ulysses Lee. "[African Americans] had been used in a wider range of geographical, cultural, and climatic conditions than was believed possible." Of the 2.5 million Black people who registered for the draft, a little more than 900,000 served in the army, or about 9 percent. A little over 2 percent of the marines were Black, or about 17,000 troops.

Prior to 1941, it was our country's policy to maintain segregated military units in all the armed forces. With very few exceptions, White officers were in charge of Blacks, and Black officers weren't given much responsibility. One of the great stories of World War II was of the brave and successful all-Black air squadron, which became known as the Tuskegee Airmen. Sixty-six would die in battle.

Although Chuck didn't question what his country might ask of him, many African Americans in the military were distraught. They wanted to defend their country, yet they were not treated equally in or out of uniform. President Franklin D. Roosevelt saw the need for Blacks both to fight and to work on the home front. Millions moved North to industrial centers where they could earn decent wages for the military build-up. As a result, Roosevelt signed an executive order just before Pearl Harbor outlawing racially discriminatory hiring practices in any defense industry. This was a benchmark event, noted by many political scientists as marking the time when Blacks started supporting the Democratic Party rather than the Republicans. It didn't take long for one of Chuck's fellow Black sailors to make history. Dorie Miller shot down at least two Japanese attacking planes at Pearl Harbor, possibly saving hundreds or thousands of lives. He did this even though he had been prohibited from being in combat. He was supposed to be working in the ship kitchen, but with Japanese planes attacking from every side, Miller decided to take the situation and the big guns in his own hands.

He was honored for his bravery about a year later, but toward the end of the war he was killed when a Japanese submarine sank his ship. His officers had put him back to work in the kitchen.

Chuck would have liked to have been in the fighting, too. But he ended up playing a lot of ball. His talent entertained a lot of fighting men. Years ago, he explained to Brent Kelly: "We had a basketball team at Great Lakes and also a baseball team. Of course, it was a Black team. Back then you couldn't play sports with the Whites in the service." Not fighting directly for his country was troublesome. "You go in the service to fight for your country, then you're segregated. They had what they called the Black navy and the White navy. The army was the same way." Chuck thinks it's ironic that the military would not let him compete with many of the White players he played against in high school and college. "It was funny how you could do something one day and you couldn't the next."

Navy football players were treated differently than the basketball and baseball players. That may have been due to the resolve of Paul Brown, Ohio's famous football coach, who created the Cincinnati Bengals. Blacks could play on Brown's gridiron teams but not the other sports. One of his assistants for the Great Lakes team was Steve Belichick, father of super-bowl-winning Bill Belichick of the New England Patriots. Great Lakes was considered a college team and went 10–2 with a 19 to 14 win over top-ranked Notre Dame. Buddy Young and Marion Motley played on those teams and became top professionals.

Chuck played with the great Larry Doby on both the navy basketball and baseball teams. Doby was a second-generation veteran who had to sit on the bench. His dad, David Doby, had been a groom for horses in World War I. Harmon and Doby lived in separate barracks from the Whites and could play only with and against other Black players. "If you would have said something in the navy," Harmon told writer Steve Jacobson years ago, "it was mutiny and they could put you in the brig."

Still, University of Kentucky legendary coach Adolph Rupp said that the navy basketball team that included Harmon and Doby was the greatest team he had ever seen, college or professional. Chuck just laughs and says old Adolph "must have been talking about the White team."

World War II ended in victory, and the Black soldiers and workers back home had played a significant role. But obviously, the struggle was far from over. Many Blacks were barred from victory parades and segregated at canteens, in some churches, and when they were transported. They had fought to save freedom and equality for America when they didn't have it themselves. That was true, for the most part, in the military, and it certainly was a fact in professional baseball.

That's why many African Americans in post-World War II America said, "Thank God for the Negro Leagues."

The Negro Leagues

Chuck Harmon has one of the shortest and strangest stories from his days in the Negro Leagues. There are many stars and stories from those glorious leagues. No question, many Black players would have been great major leaguers had they been given the opportunity, and that means many average White players would have not had a cup of coffee in the big time.

Chuck played only five games in the Negro Leagues, and he did it under a fake name, Charlie Fine. He did that because he wanted to keep his eligibility at the University of Toledo. But he also wanted to make some money in the summer of 1947, and he couldn't get a job around the campus. A job as an outfielder with the Indianapolis Clowns in the Negro American League became available.

"I was supposed to get a job in the recreation department, but it didn't happen," Chuck remembers. Hank Rigney from the Negro Leagues lived around there [Toledo]. He was [a] scout. He asked me if I wanted to play with the Indianapolis Clowns. I needed the money." Chuck's Toledo coaches didn't know. That's why he wanted to be called somebody else. For about $150, he took off for Indy.

The Clowns were originally the Miami Giants, then the Ethiopian Clowns, and then the Indianapolis Clowns. Later, the franchise would be shared by Cincinnati and Indianapolis. If it weren't a serious league game, the Clowns would play baseball like the Harlem Globetrotters play basketball, with lots of entertaining tricks and showmanship. Today, Chuck has a hard time remembering just what happened in his five-game career in the league, but he does remember meeting the team and playing against the Kansas City Monarchs.

In an interview years ago with Brent Kelley, he had a clearer memory of those days. He confirms this is what he said: "Right after the game with the Monarchs we left to go to Flint, Michigan, to play on Thursday. I think we played the Monarchs up there. You ride up there all night and part of the next day to get there and you get up there at nine or ten o'clock on Thursday, then right after the game that night you get on the bus and we went to Fort Wayne, Indiana, to play Friday night." From there, it was Michigan City, Indiana, and then to Chicago to play a doubleheader with the Chicago American Giants at Comiskey Park.

"I don't know, I may have batted once, pinch run, or played the outfield or something.… I decided this wasn't for me. Being in college, you traveled first class on trains and stayed in the best hotels, so I told the general manager that I was gonna leave the team," he said. That worked out well because there was a telegram back at his sister's house in Indianapolis from the athletic director at Toledo saying he had found that summer job close to campus.

He is very clear on a couple of things. He remembers how uncomfortable he was in the back of the team bus, and he remembers how he got his fake name. "The regulars get a seat in front by themselves. You gotta sleep on the bus. You just sit wherever you can."

But one fellow took Chuck under his wing, Goose Tatum, a basketball star in the winter for the Harlem Globetrotters. He gave Chuck his fake name and sometimes let him sit with him in the big seat up front. "He didn't want me to get in trouble and be ineligible for college."

To this day, Chuck wishes he could have played a season or so in the Negro Leagues to see the great players, crowds, and to see how he would have faired. In the end, it didn't matter, because Jackie opened the door that year and Chuck would soon sign to play professional baseball in a league that had previously banned Black players.

Marvelous in the Minors

Pete Rose once said he would walk through hell in a gasoline suit to play baseball. Chuck could relate to the Rose kid, who used to hang out around Crosley Field before and after Reds games. Like Rose, he never really met a baseball game he didn't like. "I loved to play. Who wouldn't?"

Chuck's minor league career is long and storied. The numbers in the back of the book show just how well he did in most of his fifteen years of professional baseball, especially in the minors. The typically humble Harmon says, "I always did well." He made one of those famous Willie Mays' over-the-head, facing-the-opposite way catches before Willie made it famous in the big leagues. Around the small minor league parks across the country, there was always a lot of talk about Chuck Harmon.

He was a great minor league player and a fair major league player who may have never gotten the opportunity he deserved. After that, he went back to the minors and did quite well again, playing ball and reaping some financial rewards.

His professional career began after his days at the University of Toledo and his short stint in the Negro Leagues. The St. Louis Browns had a minor league team in Toledo, and that's where the scouts discovered the Harmon kid was just as good with the bat and glove as he was with his basketball jump shot and defense. The Browns played in St. Louis from 1902 to 1953, when they became the Baltimore Orioles.

Jackie had opened the door, and Chuck was ready to carry the torch. He signed with St. Louis and was ready to go play … immediately. "I thought I would go straight to the Browns, but the same day I signed Willard Brown and Hank Thompson signed in St. Louis and got to stay," Chuck remembered. "They sent me to upstate New York to play at Gloversville in the minors."

He was the first Black player there. The local paper said he was "a Negro star sent here Saturday by the parent St. Louis Browns." He turned out to be a very good and popular player for the Electrics.

Chuck's baseball odyssey is a bit confusing. He could still play some basketball at Toledo because of what he had missed during the war. He explains, "In 1948 they changed the rule about being a pro. [Previously, if you were] a pro in one sport, you [were] a pro in all.… In 1948, the NCAA changed the rules, but they gave everybody in college [who] was playing another sport [permission] to go ahead and play." Thus, in 1948 and 1949, Chuck went back to playing basketball at Toledo and skipped a lot of baseball. He left the St. Louis Browns behind. The Rockets would never have the success they'd had his freshman year, but they were a national power.

He did make some baseball history in Ft. Wayne. "There was a semi-pro baseball team there. I tried out and made it. I was the only Black on the team.… We had a pretty good ball club with several ex-major leaguers.… When I was with Gloversville, I was making $175 or $200 a month.… I was making more playing semi-pro baseball, and I was still eligible for college." But soon it was back to Gloversville, and baseball and his new bride Pearl were the main objects of Harmon's attention.

"I had good years," he recalls, ".375 or something like that each year and around 140 hits both years. So, for 1952, they sold my contract to the Reds and they sent me to Toledo." By this time the Browns had been sold and the Reds made Toledo one of their farm teams. He went to Tulsa in the Texas League. He was just one step away from being the first Black Red. It was there that he and his light-skinned wife faced prejudice in and out of the ballpark. "It hurt, but what are you going to do?"

Technically, he was on the Reds roster at the end of the 1953 season and may have been called up, but word was the manager at the time didn't want a Black on his team. "He didn't care for Blacks so the Reds wouldn't bring me up." The manager's name was Rogers Hornsby, one of the greatest players of all time. His lifetime batting average of .358 is second all-time behind Ty Cobb's .367. Luckily for Chuck, the Reds players couldn't stand Hornsby, and he was fired just in time for Chuck to plan for a fresh start at spring training with new manager George "Birdie" Tebbetts.

To prepare Chuck for the big time and the opportunity to be the first African American on the Reds, the club sent him on a baseball vacation. "They sent me to [play] winter ball down in Puerto Rico, and I hit about .327," Chuck says. "I think I was second in the league in hitting. That's when I ran into Hank Aaron. He finished three points under me in batting." It was just what the baseball doctor ordered—stiff competition.

"They had a lot of hard throwers down there. Jack Harshman, left-hander for the White Sox; Karl Spooner, left-hander for the Dodgers. Howie Judson pitched for us. It was a really good league, and that made it almost sure I was gonna make the Reds. All I had to do was do a little something in spring training."

The stage was set. It was time for history to be made.

Major League Pioneer

Rookie Season: The 1954 Slamming Redlegs

THE 1954 REDS WERE A FASCINATING BUNCH. They had sluggers like Ted Kluszewski, who became the first Red to lead the league in home runs and RBIs in the same season. They had a darn good pitcher by the name of Joe Nuxhall. There was a great compliment of players, including Gus Bell, Wally Post, and Roy McMillan. And there was the dark-skinned rookie, Chuck Harmon. If Chuck could do just a portion for the Reds what Jackie Robinson had done for the Dodgers and Willie Mays had done for the Giants, the Reds' decision to cross the color line would not be questioned.

Many times during the 1954 season, Chuck would lead off and play third base. He was known as a solid contact hitter with excellent speed. If you study the written play-by-play accounts, nearly every time out on the field, Chuck and the Reds were taking on eventual Hall of Famers. Of course, there was Jackie with the Dodgers. Willie with the Giants. But the Cubs had Ernie Banks. The Braves had Hank Aaron. The Cardinals had Stan Musial.

Chuck can be very proud. He held his own. In fact, if you look closely, about half the time when he faced off against the stars he did as well or better. But his season would run hot and cold, and it seemed Manager

Birdie Tebbetts would bench Chuck for no apparent reason, many times after he was on a hitting tear. But it's been too many years too complain. Chuck's glad he had what chance he did.

"I wondered how I [w]ould have played if I had known I had a job, but I never did. [B]all players always want to play, but I've wondered if my skin was part of the decision process."

Still, Chuck was a major part of the Reds' mid-season surge. They were 47–41 on July 19, 1954, and looked like they were in the pennant chase and would have their first winning season in a decade. Let's take a close look at what happened that season. For more specific numbers, refer to the statistics in the back of the book or read the timeline earlier in this book.

"I did pretty well in spring training," Chuck says. "I wasn't a home-run hitter—oh, I always hit a few—but I'd usually get you in. I was the fastest on the team." All during his rookie season, he never felt like he could have the job as the Reds' third baseman. Oh, he started and led off quite a bit, but he felt like he was being jerked around a bit. "It's all fine now," he says. "The Reds have been great to me, but looking back then, I would have liked them to say the job was mine. I was one of those guys, I had to play, I never could hit my eye platooning and playing here and there."

When they headed north, Tebbetts warned Chuck to remain calm when he heard insults or when other players tried to start something. He said, "Walk away, fold yours arms. If not, you'll get beat up and blamed for starting it," Chuck remembered in an interview with Steve Jacobson. The season started and Chuck sat on the bench for four days and then became the first African American to play for the Reds. It was April 17, 1954, just sky of his thirtieth birthday. Chuck wasn't a young rookie.

It was a bright, cool day in Milwaukee. He pinched hit and popped out in the seventh inning. The Reds lost 5 to 1. History had been made; now it was up to Chuck to keep it going. On May 5 he got to start and led off against Willie Mays and the Giants. He responded with two hits in a 7 to 1 win. He would then go 3–10 in the next few games before taking a seat on the bench for a while. It would be a pattern he would face much of the season.

"I was always in and out of the lineup. Bobby Adams and myself, we used to tease each other. I would go out there and have a big day, or he would, and the next day we'd say, well, 'you're out of the lineup.'"

Chuck is still proud of many games during his rookie season. In head-to-head matchups that year with Jackie and the Dodgers, Hank and the Braves, Willie and the Giants, and Stan and the Cardinals, he did very well. It would be his best professional year, but some things really stick out:

- His first home run off Hall of Famer Warren Spahn: "I didn't really see it go out; I just heard the crowd and started running around the bases."
- His many three- and four-hit days
- A dramatic winning hit against Philadelphia
- Four hits in a 14 to 4 blowout of Willie and the Giants

His favorite day may have been Chuck Harmon Day, August 29, 1954. A train brought family and friends from his hometown of Washington. His mom and dad made it, as did many of his sisters, brothers, and friends. "I had three hits, and my mom and dad got to see it," he says. "That was a good day." Chuck would finish the season with a lot of bench time. As late as 2010 when asked why, Chuck would point at the skin on his wrist and rub. But it doesn't take long for a smile to come out, and all he can say is how thankful he was that got to be there.

After many high hopes in the spring, the Reds would finish with seventy-four wins and eighty losses, fifth place in the National League. Chuck played in ninety-four games and hoped for a better year to come.

The 1955 Reds

The Reds looked to have more pitching to go with their slammers as they headed for spring camp in Tampa. Chuck had to stay in a boarding house near the baseball facility. One of his housemates was Curt Flood, the future St. Louis Cardinal who would make history in his legal battles with Major League Baseball. Years later, Reds manager Gabe Paul told Chuck's son Charlie, "Your father and I went through a lot of stuff." Nevertheless, Chuck was back for a second year.

The Reds got off to a horrible start. They limped to a 4–13 start and never really got on track. Oh, Klu hit forty-seven home runs and Post, Temple, and Bell played well, but it was a difficult year for fierce competitors like Chuck Harmon. He played in ninety-six Reds games, two more than the previous season. And he actually hit the ball a lot better, but there was the old business of sitting him down when it seemed he might play consistently. Was it because he was Black? We'll never know.

He got the nickname "the Glove" because he could play just about any position, and he had a special glove to go with each one. He spent most of the time staying at an all-Black hotel and, more times than not, eating at Black-only restaurants. "The White players didn't know we weren't staying with them most of the time." The plan was to play hard, be quiet, keep his head down, and not cause trouble, no matter how frustrated he was.

Things took a serious turn for Chuck on July 23, 1955. He broke up a no-hitter against the Giants at New York's Polo Grounds. Jim Hearn was two outs away from history. "Tebbetts sent me up to pinch-hit with one out in the bottom of the ninth," says Chuck. "I hit a dying quail over the head of shortstop Alvin Dark. It was the only hit we got in the game. I got a letter from a New York fan who said he was going to shoot me when I walked on the field at New York."

The letter was turned over to the FBI. They would be back at the ballpark when Chuck decided not to worry. "The clubhouses were in the centerfield in the Polo Grounds, and when it was time for us to go out on the field, before the game, I walked down the steps between the bleachers with Wally Post and Gus Bell. We got to the field and, they said, 'Oh man, Chuck's supposed to get shot today. What are we doing?' They ran about twenty feet away; they were kidding. They came over and walked the rest of the way in right next to me. I appreciated that."

Chuck had one of the best quotes of the 1955 season when the media asked if he was scared that day. "Not really," he said. "I figured [that] if the guy who'd sent me the death threat were a true New York fan, he wouldn't dare shoot me. If he did, our manager would put somebody in the lineup that could really hit, and it would hurt the Giants worse than me."

1956 Cincinnati Reds

Things would get tougher for Chuck. He knew he could play, but he felt his opportunity would be less and less. A key reason was that Frank

Robinson became the second African American to play for the Reds. He was sensational. "There was always talk of a quota," says Chuck. "You know, scouts or coaches or managers would say you can only have so many Blacks."

Chuck would bat only thirteen times for the Reds in 1956. On May 16, he was traded to the St. Louis Cardinals for Alex Grammas and Joe Frazier. The Reds would go on to have a great year and fall just short in the pennant race. For Chuck, success would remain elusive. He batted only twenty times for the Cardinals. With injuries and a lack of playing time, he was in only nine games the next year, before the Cards traded him to the Philadelphia Phillies on September 15, 1957.

He played pretty well for the Phillies, hitting .258, but once the season was over, he never made it back up. Instead, he played four more years in the minors, hitting well and teaching young players the finer points of the game. He knew it was time to quit when he was playing for the Hawaii Islanders in 1961. He was thirty-seven. "You know, at some point, you say, that's it. I was there."

Thoughts on Pete & Marge
& the Reds Today

Chuck Harmon is so very nice and soft spoken about so many things that you almost want to send out a media alert when he is direct and edgy. He's fiercely loyal to a few people he has passed along life's highway, and they would include Pete Rose, Marge Schott, and Ken Griffey Jr.

Chuck was cast into the spotlight in 1990 when I interviewed him about Eric Davis's allegation that race was a factor in Marge Schott's actions as majority owner. Chuck didn't think so. In fact, he thought Marge was discriminated against because she was a woman in a man's game, both as a baseball owner and as a car dealer.

"Marge and I got along real good," Chuck said while sitting in his box seats at Great American Ballpark. "Everybody would talk about how she was prejudiced and everything like that but, no, [she] was all right. She invited me to a lot of things. I was thankful for whatever they did for me. They did what they could, and I loved every minute. But a lot of people didn't like Marge. I hate to say it, but a big part of that was because she was a woman and pulled the strings. A lot of people don't like women doing that."

Chuck says Marge stood tall after her husband died and refused to give up the family car dealerships. "A lot of men love the women, but they want

145

their finger holding them down. She built up those dealership businesses, and she was good for the baseball team. It was hard for her to deal with men owners, sitting back with their cigars, but she was a tough business woman."

And Pete Rose? "He is like one of my kids. I knew Pete since he was little hanging around the ballpark with this parents." Chuck has nothing but admiration for the baseball's all-time hit leader. Pete checks on him at the ballpark to see how he's doing. After baseball when Chuck was working for McGregor Sports, Pete was one of his clients. Chuck's job was to keep Pete and other clients, like Willie Mays, happy and wanting to keep their names on gloves.

"If anybody should be in the Hall of Fame, it's Pete Rose," says Chuck. "The records he set, nobody's going to break them." He believes Pete's gambling on baseball should be forgiven. He believes Pete never bet on the Reds to lose and never did anything to change the outcome of a game.

"I don't believe it. I don't think he would do anything to jeopardize the game. Pete did more for baseball than just about anybody. There are only six or seven players who ever played who did as much for the game as Pete, on the field or off the field."

Chuck says Pete still could be a great ambassador for the game. "You get him in a crowd and there is no one better to stimulate people. They want to listen to him. He's witty, just funny, and he knows what he is talking about. He knows everything about baseball. It's worth your money to go and be around him.

"If it were up to me, he'd have been in the Hall of Fame long time ago. You got all these guys taking steroids and stuff, and they're not saying much about them. As hard-nosed as Pete Rose was about baseball, he would never do anything to hurt the game. And if you really know Pete Rose, money doesn't mean much to him. I'd like to see him come back as a manager again. He could inspire players. A lot of young players seem like they don't care; they don't run hard on pop ups or ground balls." Harmon is referring here to "Charlie Hustle," who was famous for running to first even after a walk.

"The way Pete always hustled, he would inspire them now." The bottom line, Chuck says, is that betting didn't make Pete a better player, Pete did. "Hell, yes. He's still gotta play."

PLAY ON

Chuck lives these days for the Cincinnati Reds.

He looks forward to every home game he can attend. Cataracts on his eyes have slowed him down, so he always needs a ride to the Reds new ballpark down by the river, the place that feels almost more home than home now that Pearl is gone.

It has been a long way from old Allen Field in Washington, Indiana to the Great American baseball palace in Cincinnati.

He is so proud of that park, the team, its history, and the part he played in it. He is so thankful to Reds management and the fans who treat him so nicely and with such great respect.

He looks at the beauty of Great American Ball Park, and is amazed at the difference between it and the places he played years ago. "Some places were like goat paths," he laughs. "You never knew what a ball would do," he said, referring to infields and outfields scattered with dips, rocks, and a few surprising valleys that might help make a slow roller become a face smasher; although he admits he learned to play the old terrace at Crosley Field pretty well, while many visiting players could never figure out why the outfield suddenly ramped up to the wall.

His life flew by so quickly.

Times are so different.

Many of those he played with are gone now. After telling or listening to stories, Chuck many times asks, "are they still alive?" Most are not.

He traveled in cars, hot buses, trains, and a few jet planes. But he didn't enjoy anything close to the luxuries of today's professional stars who make mind-boggling money and travel like rock stars.

However, he sure is glad he played a role in establishing the lifestyle enjoyed today by some of the world's greatest athletes. "I think they deserve it. Look how difficult it is to get there. Look how few get there."

He doesn't mind if the new players don't care to get to know him, though most of them eventually do. He likes it when the young guys remember people like Jackie Robinson, and sometimes, Chuck Harmon, but he says that's not the point.

"Just so today's players know they didn't start everything. It was not a piece of cake for us...White players had to worry about the curve ball, we had some other things on our minds, too."

But it's rare that Chuck ever has even a slight edge in his conversation. He is fine with it if people remember him or if they don't. He hopes when people do remember him, they will think of him as a man who played and lived with integrity. He really doesn't care if they remember the color of his skin.

However, Reds Team Historian Greg Rhodes said Chuck's role was special, and we should strive to remember.

"The Reds were slow to integrate, seven years after Jackie Robinson. By the time guys like Chuck came along, they (players like Chuck) didn't get a lot of attention, like Robinson and the first few guys.

But Rhodes said that doesn't diminish what Chuck accomplished or went through.

"Cincinnati was the Southernmost town, and there was quite a bit of hostility. Chuck doesn't dwell on that, but Cincinnati was still a segregated town back then. Players had to endure a lot, and their families."

Rhodes said Chuck Harmon will always be an important part of Reds history.

"He really stood for something for the Reds. It's a more significant milestone today than when he played. He is more appreciated today. In part, because of the way he's carried himself. He has done nothing but make fans out of people who never saw him play. "

Chuck said he hopes President Obama does a good job, because – at the end of the life's game - it doesn't matter the most who was the first African American president. Chuck said the most significant thing is that there will be many Black presidents, and eventually, that nobody will be watching and counting color at all, because we will be as one. This coming from a guy who has spent most of his life as a Republican. But that was before Barack.

It reminds us of how Jackie Robinson opened the door for people like Chuck, and Chuck made sure the door would stay open for other great leaders in the game of baseball. Now, nobody in baseball pays that much attention to the color. They look more for character and ability.

Maybe that's fine and dandy. We need baseball for other reasons.

We have the economy to worry about. We have wars to keep us on our toes. We have plenty of blowhard politicians, bankers, and oil barons to fear and cause us to fear each other.

Why not sports to help us escape reality and live a dream?

A dream that was Chuck Harmon's life.

Just the other day I was lucky to meet Kit O'Meara, the daughter of possibly the greatest sportswriters ever, Red Smith of the New York Times. The occasion was the dedication of the sportswriters hall of fame in her dad's name at Indiana University's National Sports Journalism Center.

She seemed excited to hear more about Chuck Harmon and his story. Her dad, whom she called Pop, was one of the first to tell the world about the excellence of Jackie Robinson, and the absurdity of a color ban.

Her dad wrote a story on Robinson when he was playing in the minor leagues in Montreal. It appeared August 4, 1946, the fall before he would break the color line by being called up by the Dodgers.

Jackie told Red Smith he had great hope for the future. Imagine him thinking that after his Montreal manager had suggested when he was traded there that Blacks weren't human beings.

Jackie told Red Smith Black kids used to give up on playing sports, figuring – like everything in life – there was no opportunity. "Now, I think they'll produce more good players," Jackie told Red months before making history. One of those good players to follow was Chuck.

After Jackie died, Red Smith talked of Robinson being "the unconquerable doing the impossible."

This is the kind of legacy left behind by men like Jackie and Chuck. Because of that, we see something special in baseball; an island of beauty in our stormy, unpredictable world.

One May a few years after he helped break the color barrier by signing Jackie, Branch Rickey, a man Red Smith called a "friend" and a "fighter," said there would always be great things to be found in baseball.

"Baseball is a game of great charm, in the adoptions of mathematical measurements to the timing of human movements, the exactitudes and adjustments of physical ability to hazardous chance. The speed of the leg, the dexterity of the body, the grace of the swing, the elusiveness of the slide – these are the features that make Americans everywhere forget the last syllable of a man's last name or the pigmentation of his skin."

So true.

Play on.

Epilogue

We're just talking about sports, right?

In many of the newspaper, radio, and television newsrooms across America, they refer to the sports department as the "toy department." Professionally speaking, I've shopped a lot in both.

As a reporter, I've covered 9/11 and a few other disasters, but I've been at the World Series, the NCAA Final Four, and the Super Bowl.

The theory among some old, crusty, print-stained journalists, is that writing or talking about sports is not that serious; it's just a bunch of games. Studies show that only about one in four people really, really, care about sports most of the time, but then there are those other times.

The news and sports media line has been blurred many times in the last few years with issues surrounding steroids, gambling basketball referees, and the love lives of golfers. If you believe my old acquaintance, Bob Knight, there are a lot of naughty things going on in big-time college basketball. Should we all find something else to do and stop letting sports break our hearts like a love we can't let go? Well, no.

It's important to go back full circle. With all the ugly reality in sports, how refreshing it is to see something like a bunch of high-school kids battling for the pride of their community, or a small college taking on an NBA factory for the national championship, or a baseball team people have loved since 1869 go for another championship. If your team doesn't win, it's a shame, but it's not the end of the world.

Chuck and I had some positive sports karma in 2010. We got to go back and see his old high school win a state title again at the NBA field house in Indianapolis. We followed Butler University to the NCAA basketball finals and visited their old home, Hinkle Fieldhouse, a place where Chuck was 4 and 0 as a player. Then there was the start of the Reds season.

As I was hanging around home plate with other media types waiting for the first pitch of 2010 in Cincinnati, I was mesmerized by the beautiful green grass and perfect lime lines. There was Johnny Bench, the greatest catcher of all time, his hat backward like a college kid's, playing around with a baseball, smiling like a little leaguer who knows, no matter what, he's going to have fun and the coach is going to buy him a snow cone after the game.

Yeah, it's just a bunch of games. But sometimes, because of the games and the people we watch play them, like a Jackie Robinson or Chuck Harmon, the world is miraculously changed for the better. Those men helped make a mockery of hate. Today they remind us anything is possible, and if you can't make it, isn't it a blast to watch others try to climb the mountain?

If nothing else, thank God we have the games to escape grown men and women wrestling like demons over healthcare, nuclear weapons, and immigration. God bless the boys and girls of summer, fall, winter, and spring.

An Essay on American Life

By Charles B. Harmon

My feelings about living in the United States of America can be summarized in one word: GREAT!

Being free to live, work, and raise a family is what makes this country great. Why do we need a catastrophe to awaken us from our dilemmas, to be kind, thoughtful, loving, considerate, and sympathetic to one another? Does our self-centeredness blind us to our surroundings and limit our minds to superficial things?

Thousands of immigrants flock to this great land everyday, some legally and some illegally, but all seeking a new way of life. Even people who criticize the United States rarely try to escape this peace-loving land to go elsewhere. Nevertheless, many Americans take what we have for granted, and that imposes on each of us an obligation of endurance and tolerance. We need to reach out and embrace each other and the people of other countries and to work harder to understand and communicate with each other. Only then can we learn that we have much in common, that we want many of the same things for our families and for our countries.

Growing up in the United States was one of the luckiest things to happen to me. Being Black and poor can be a big obstacle in life. But how

I approached these obstacles and dealt with them helped me to develop common sense and a way to solve problems that has maintained me throughout my life.

Being the tenth of twelve children in my family meant that I was always at the bottom of the list. It was difficult for my parents, Sherman and Rosa Harmon, to raise a family that large through the difficult times of the 1920s and 1930s. But both of my parents had taught school early in life, and they made sure that each of us graduated from high school and saw nine of us attend college. With the help of God and the church, my parents created strong bonds among the members of our family. It is a tribute to my parents that those bonds remain strong to this day.

With my country, I have lived through a lot of changes, including the 1929 stock market crash, the Great Depression, the Japanese attack on Pearl Harbor, the Second World War (during which I served in the navy), the conflicts in Korea and Vietnam (through which my wife, Daurel, and I raised our three children), and most recently, the September 11, 2001, terrorist attacks on the World Trade Center and the Pentagon. I am concerned when I hear that U.S. citizens have sold out our country by disclosing to other governments our confidential secrets, or that our own government has endangered its people by disclosing too much information or by ignoring the threat posed by the presence of people of questionable character in this country.

Looking back over my lifetime, however, I am confident in our country's ability to endure any emergency. Throughout its history, the United States has remained a free nation. I am very proud and honored to call myself an American and to have been able to raise my family in this great country of ours, just as my parents did.

My life has taught me the importance of self respect and respect for others. Everyone wants to get ahead in this world, but those efforts may fail. Most people do not plan to fail, but they fail to plan. Thus I have learned to plan ahead and map out different situations to guide me in the direction that best suits my ideas and me. But I have also learned to diversify, so that, no matter what obstacle presents itself, I can at least avert a major disaster. And I have learned to be flexible, to adjust and be adaptable to changes. Finally, experience has taught me to help others less fortunate than myself.

I believe that we, as citizens of this country, owe it to our country to abide by its rules. If we could live our lives by a strict code of personal and public ethics, the whole world would profit with dignity, humility, and a sense of purpose. There would be less bloodshed and more peace and harmony in the world.

Through the years, growing up in a small town in the Midwest, playing high school and college basketball, serving my country in the navy during World War II, playing the grand old game of baseball in (and a role in the integration of) the major leagues, I have met people from all walks of life. It has been an experience beyond my wildest dreams. Only in America, thank God!

FIRST MODERN AFRICAN AMERICAN MAJOR LEAGUE BASEBALL PLAYERS

PLAYER	TEAM	DATE
Jackie Robinson	Brooklyn Dodgers, NL	April 15, 1947
Larry Doby	Cleveland Indians, AL	July 5, 1947
Hank Thompson	St. Louis Browns, AL	July 17, 1947
Roy Campanella	Brooklyn Dodgers, NL	April 20, 1948
Don Newcombe	Brooklyn Dodgers, NL	May 20, 1949
Monte Irvin	New York Giants, NL	July 8, 1949
Hank Thompson	New York Giants, NL	July 8, 1949
Sam Jethroe	Boston Braves, NL	April 18, 1950
Minnie Minoso	Chicago White Sox, AL	May 1, 1951
Willie Mays	New York Giants, NL	May 25, 1951
Bob Trice	Philadelphia Athletics, AL	September 13, 1953
Ernie Banks	Chicago Cubs, NL	September 17, 1953
Hank Aaron	Milwaukee Braves, NL	April 13, 1954
Curt Roberts	Pittsburgh Pirates, NL	April 13, 1954
Tom Alston	St. Louis Cardinals, NL	April 13, 1954
Chuck Harmon	Cincinnati Reds, NL	April 17, 1954
Carlos Paula	Washington Senators, AL	September 6, 1954
Elston Howard	New York Yankees, AL	April 14, 1955
John Kennedy	Philadelphia Phillies, NL	April 22, 1957
Ozzie Virgil, Sr.	Detroit Tigers, AL	June 6, 1958
Pumpsie Green	Boston Red Sox, AL	July 21 1959

CAREER STATISTICS

CHARLES (CHUCK) BYRON HARMON
Nicknames: Charlie Fine, The Glove
Born: April 23, 1924   Washington, IN
Ht. 6' 2"   Wt. 175   Batted and Threw R

Year	Team, (Affiliation) League	Pos	G	AB	R	H	2B	3B	HR	RBI	SB	BA
1947	Indianapolis (IN) Clowns, NegroAmL	OF	5	Other Statistics Not Available								
1947	Gloversville (NY) Glovers, (Browns) CanAmL	OF	64	200	24	54	10	1	0	29	6	.270
1948	Played for the Ft. Wayne General Electric Semi-Pro National Champs											
1949	Gloversville (NY) Glovers, (Browns) CanAmL	OF	14	51	3	11	1	2	0	7	0	.216
1949	Olean (NY) Oilers, (Browns) PONY	OF 3B	31	134	20	47	12	1	1	21	0	.351
1949	Gloversville / Olean Combined	OF 3B	45	185	23	58	13	3	1	28	0	.314
1950	Olean (NY) Oilers, (No Affiliation) PONY	1B 3B SS	125	551	125	206	47	10	22	139	17	.374
1951	Olean (NY) Oilers, (No Affiliation) PONY	1B 3B SS	113	467	107	175	37	10	15	143	25	.375
1952	Burlington (IA) Flints, (Reds) IIIL	OF 3B	124	479	97	153	34	6	5	71	43	.319
1953	Tulsa (OK) Oilers, (Reds) TxL	OF 3B	143	566	86	176	24	11	14	83	24	.311
1954	Cincinnati, NL	1B 3B	94	286	39	68	7	3	2	25	7	.238
1955	Cincinnati, NL	OF 1B 3B	96	198	31	50	6	3	5	28	9	.253
1956	Cincinnati, NL	OF 1B	13	4	2	0	0	0	0	0	1	.000
1956	St. Louis, NL	OF 1B 3B	20	15	2	0	0	0	0	0	0	.000
1956	Cincinnati / St. Louis Totals	OF 1B 3B	33	19	4	0	0	0	0	0	1	.000
1956	Omaha (NB) Cardinals, (Cardinals) AA	OF	58	242	50	87	17	6	10	49	4	.360
1957	St. Louis, NL	OF	9	3	2	1	0	1	0	1	1	.333
1957	Philadelphia, NL	OF 1B 3B	57	86	14	22	2	1	0	5	7	.256
1957	St. Louis / Philadelphia Combined	OF 1B 3B	66	89	16	23	2	2	0	6	8	.258
1958	Miami (FL) Marlins, (Phillies) IntL	OF 3B	36	126	12	26	2	2	0	11	4	.206
1958	St. Paul (MN) Saints, (Dodgers) AA	OF 3B	38	143	18	41	4	2	0	9	1	.287
1958	Miami / St. Paul Combined	OF 3B	74	269	30	67	6	4	0	20	5	.249
1959	Charleston (WV) Senators, (Tigers) AA	OF	20	65	9	15	3	1	4	11	0	.231
1959	Salt Lake City (UT) Bees, (Pirates) PCL	OF	118	449	64	139	22	9	7	90	9	.310
1959	Charleston / Salt Lake City Combined	OF	138	514	73	154	25	10	11	101	9	.300
1960	Salt Lake City (UT) Bees, (Pirates) PCL	OF	136	415	57	119	15	7	4	35	10	.287
1961	Hawaii Islanders, (Athletics) PCL	OF INF	7	23	3	4	0	0	0	1	1	.174
	Major League Totals	OF 1B 3B	289	592	90	141	15	8	7	59	25	.238
	Minor League Totals	OF INF	1027	3911	675	1253	228	68	82	699	144	.320
	1953-54 Ponce, PR Lions PRWL	3B	70	269	36	88	5	7	1	23	9	.327
	1955-56 Ponce, PR Lions PRWL	3B		278		82			5	26		.295
	Puerto Rico Winter League Totals	3B		547		170			6	49		.311

Signed as an amateur free agent by St. Louis Browns 1947

Returned to Oleans Oilers by St. Louis Browns after the end of their minor league working agreement, 1950

Signed by Cincinnati Reds, 1952

Traded by Cincinnati Reds to St. Louis Cardinals in exchange for Joe Frazier and Alex Grammas, May 16, 1956

Traded by St. Louis Cardinals to Philadelphia Philles in exchange for Glen Gorbous, May 10, 1957

MLB Debut: April 17, 1954, Cincinnati Reds

Last MLB Game: September 15, 1957, Philadelphia Phillies

Also played in the Domincan League in the 1958-59 and 1959-60 seasons

Chuck Harmon 1954 Cincinnati Batting Log

Date	#	Opponent	GS	AB	R	H	2B	3B	HR	RBI	BB	IBB	SO	HBP	SH	SF	GDP	SB	CS	AVG	OBP	SLG	BP	Pos
04/17/54		AT MIL N	0	1	0	0	0	0	0	0	0	0	0	0	0	0	0	0	0	.000	.000	.000	9	ph
04/19/54		AT STL N	0	1	0	0	0	0	0	1	0	0	0	0	0	1	0	0	0	.000	.000	.000	9	ph, 3b
04/21/54		VS STL N	0	1	0	0	0	0	0	0	0	0	1	0	0	0	0	0	0	.000	.000	.000	9	ph
04/25/54	1	VS CHI N	0	1	0	0	0	0	0	0	0	0	0	0	0	0	0	0	0	.000	.000	.000	9	ph
04/25/54	2	VS CHI N	1	4	1	2	1	0	0	0	1	0	0	0	0	0	0	0	0	.250	.300	.375	1	3b
04/27/54		VS PIT N	1	3	1	0	0	0	0	0	1	0	0	0	0	0	0	0	0	.182	.286	.273	1	3b
04/28/54		VS PIT N	1	4	1	2	1	0	0	0	0	0	0	0	0	0	0	0	0	.267	.333	.400	1	3b
04/30/54		VS BRO N	1	1	0	0	0	0	0	0	0	0	0	0	0	0	0	1	0	.250	.316	.375	1	3b
05/02/54		VS PHI N	0	1	1	1	0	0	0	1	0	0	0	0	0	0	0	0	0	.294	.350	.412	9	ph
05/05/54		VS NY N	0	5	1	2	2	0	0	2	0	0	0	0	0	0	0	0	0	.318	.360	.500	8	ph
05/06/54		VS NY N	1	4	0	0	0	0	0	0	0	0	0	0	0	0	0	1	0	.269	.310	.423	1	3b
05/07/54		VS STL N	1	2	1	2	0	0	0	1	1	0	0	0	0	0	0	1	0	.321	.364	.464	1	3b
05/08/54		VS STL N	1	4	0	0	0	0	0	0	0	0	0	0	1	0	0	0	0	.281	.324	.406	4	1b
05/09/54	1	VS STL N	1	1	0	0	0	0	0	0	0	0	0	0	0	0	0	0	0	.273	.316	.394	4	1b
05/11/54		AT NY N	0	1	0	0	0	0	0	0	0	0	0	0	0	0	0	0	0	.265	.308	.382	2	ph
05/15/54		AT PHI N	0	1	0	0	0	0	0	0	0	0	0	0	0	0	0	0	0	.257	.300	.371	2	ph
05/16/54	2	AT BRO N	0	5	0	0	0	0	0	0	0	0	0	0	0	0	0	0	0	.225	.267	.325	9	ph
05/18/54		AT PIT N	1	0	0	0	0	0	0	0	0	0	0	0	0	0	0	0	0	.225	.267	.325	1	3b
05/19/54		AT PIT N	0	0	1	0	0	0	0	0	0	0	0	0	0	0	0	0	0	.225	.267	.325	8	pr
05/22/54		AT STL N	0	5	0	0	0	0	0	1	0	0	0	0	0	0	0	0	0	.200	.240	.289	5	pr
05/23/54		AT STL N	1	4	1	1	0	0	0	0	1	0	2	0	1	0	0	0	0	.204	.255	.286	1	3b
05/25/54		VS MIL N	1	1	0	1	0	0	0	0	0	0	0	0	0	0	0	0	0	.220	.268	.300	1	3b
05/26/54		VS MIL N	0	4	0	0	0	0	0	0	0	0	0	0	0	0	0	0	0	.204	.262	.278	9	ph
05/29/54		AT CHI N	1	1	0	0	0	0	0	0	1	0	0	0	0	0	0	0	0	.200	.258	.273	1	3b
05/30/54	2	AT CHI N	0	3	0	0	0	0	0	0	1	0	0	0	0	0	0	0	0	.190	.254	.259	9	ph
06/02/54		VS PHI N	1	1	0	1	0	0	0	0	0	0	0	0	0	0	0	0	0	.203	.265	.271	1	3b
06/04/54		VS NY N	0	0	0	0	0	0	0	0	1	0	0	0	0	0	0	0	0	.203	.275	.271	9	ph
06/05/54		VS NY N	1	4	0	0	0	0	0	0	0	0	1	0	0	0	0	0	0	.190	.260	.254	1	3b

DATE	GM	SITE	OPP	LG	AB	R	H	2B	3B	HR	RBI	BB	SO	SB	AVG	AVG	AVG	SP	POS
06/06/54	1	VS	NY	N	4	1	1	1	1	0	0	0	0	1	.194	.260	.269	2	3b
06/06/54	2	VS	NY	N	2	1	1	1	1	1	0	1	0	0	.203	.272	.275	2	3b
06/08/54		VS	PIT	N	4	1	1	1	0	0	0	0	0	0	.205	.271	.274	2	3b
06/09/54		VS	PIT	N	4	1	1	1	1	0	0	0	0	0	.208	.270	.273	2	3b
06/13/54	2	VS	BRO	N	4	0	1	0	1	0	0	0	0	0	.198	.258	.259	2	3b
06/15/54		AT	NY	N	0	0	0	0	0	1	0	0	0	0	.198	.258	.259	7	pr
06/16/54		AT	NY	N	3	0	1	0	1	0	0	0	0	0	.202	.260	.262	2	3b
06/17/54		AT	NY	N	4	0	0	0	0	1	0	0	0	0	.193	.250	.250	2	3b
06/22/54		AT	BRO	N	0	0	0	0	0	0	0	0	0	0	.193	.250	.250	3	1b
06/24/54		AT	BRO	N	1	0	0	0	0	0	0	0	0	0	.191	.248	.247	9	ph
06/27/54	1	AT	PIT	N	0	0	0	0	0	0	0	0	0	0	.191	.248	.247	1	3b
06/30/54		VS	STL	N	5	1	1	2	0	0	0	0	0	0	.202	.255	.277	1	3b
07/02/54	1	AT	MIL	N	0	0	0	0	1	0	1	0	0	0	.202	.255	.277	8	pr, 3b
07/07/54		AT	STL	N	5	1	1	3	0	1	0	0	0	1	.222	.270	.293	1	3b
07/08/54		AT	STL	N	4	1	1	2	0	0	0	0	0	0	.233	.278	.301	1	3b
07/09/54		VS	MIL	N	4	1	1	0	0	1	0	0	0	0	.224	.269	.290	1	3b
07/10/54		VS	MIL	N	4	1	1	3	0	0	1	0	0	0	.243	.285	.333	1	3b
07/11/54	1	VS	MIL	N	4	1	1	0	0	1	0	0	0	0	.243	.283	.330	1	3b
07/11/54	2	VS	MIL	N	5	0	0	0	0	0	1	0	0	0	.233	.273	.317	1	3b
07/15/54	1	VS	PHI	N	4	1	1	0	0	0	0	0	0	1	.226	.265	.306	1	3b
07/15/54	2	VS	PHI	N	4	1	2	2	0	0	0	0	0	0	.234	.271	.328	1	3b
07/16/54	1	VS	PHI	N	6	1	1	2	0	0	0	0	0	0	.239	.274	.328	1	3b
07/16/54	2	VS	PHI	N	5	1	2	2	0	1	0	0	0	0	.245	.278	.331	1	3b
07/17/54		VS	PHI	N	5	1	0	0	0	0	0	0	0	0	.236	.269	.319	1	3b
07/18/54	1	VS	NY	N	5	1	2	4	1	1	0	0	0	0	.255	.290	.336	1	3b
07/18/54	2	VS	NY	N	4	1	0	0	0	1	1	0	0	0	.248	.283	.327	1	3b
07/19/54		VS	NY	N	5	1	0	1	0	0	0	0	0	0	.247	.281	.323	1	3b
07/20/54		VS	NY	N	5	1	1	1	0	0	0	0	1	0	.245	.282	.319	1	3b
07/22/54		VS	BRO	N	0	0	0	0	0	1	1	0	1	0	.244	.281	.317	9	ph
07/23/54		VS	PIT	N	4	0	1	0	1	1	0	0	1	0	.238	.279	.310	2	3b

Chuck Harmon 1954 Cincinnati Batting Log

Date	#	Opponent	GS	AB	R	H	2B	3B	HR	RBI	BB	IBB	SO	HBP	SH	SF	GDP	SB	CS	AVG	OBP	SLG	BP	Pos
07/24/54		VS PIT N	1	4	1	2	0	0	0	0	0	0	0	0	0	0	0	0	0	.244	.283	.314	2	3b
07/25/54	1	VS PIT N	1	4	0	0	0	0	0	0	0	0	0	0	0	0	0	0	0	.239	.277	.307	2	3b
07/27/54		AT PHI N	1	4	0	2	0	0	0	0	0	0	0	0	0	0	0	0	0	.244	.282	.311	2	3b
07/28/54		AT PHI N	1	5	0	0	0	0	0	0	0	0	0	0	0	0	0	0	0	.238	.275	.303	2	3b
07/29/54		AT PHI N	1	5	0	1	0	0	0	0	0	0	0	0	0	0	0	0	0	.237	.273	.300	1	3b
07/30/54		AT NY N	1	4	0	1	0	0	0	0	0	0	0	0	0	0	0	0	0	.237	.273	.299	1	3b
07/31/54		AT NY N	1	4	0	0	0	0	0	0	0	0	0	0	0	0	0	0	0	.237	.272	.298	1	3b
08/01/54	1	AT NY N	1	5	1	1	0	0	0	0	0	0	0	0	0	0	0	0	0	.236	.271	.296	1	3b
08/01/54	2	AT NY N	1	3	0	0	0	0	0	0	1	0	1	0	0	0	1	0	0	.233	.270	.291	1	3b
08/03/54		AT PIT N	1	4	2	3	1	0	0	1	0	0	0	0	0	0	0	0	0	.243	.282	.305	2	3b
08/04/54		AT PIT N	1	4	1	1	0	0	0	1	0	0	1	0	0	0	0	0	0	.243	.281	.308	2	3b
08/06/54		AT BRO N	1	4	0	0	0	0	0	0	0	0	0	0	0	0	0	0	0	.239	.277	.303	2	3b
08/07/54		AT BRO N	1	4	1	1	0	0	0	0	2	0	0	0	0	0	0	0	0	.239	.276	.302	6	3b
08/08/54		AT BRO N	1	4	0	0	0	0	0	3	0	0	0	0	0	1	0	0	0	.239	.275	.301	6	3b
08/12/54		VS CHI N	0	0	0	0	0	0	0	0	0	0	0	0	0	0	0	0	0	.239	.275	.301	1	3b
08/13/54		VS STL N	0	1	0	0	0	0	0	0	0	0	0	0	0	0	0	0	0	.238	.273	.300	9	ph
08/14/54		VS STL N	1	4	0	1	0	0	0	2	1	0	0	0	0	0	0	0	1	.238	.276	.299	1	3b
08/15/54		VS STL N	1	5	2	1	0	0	0	0	0	0	0	0	0	0	0	0	0	.237	.275	.297	1	3b
08/17/54	1	AT CHI N	1	4	0	0	0	0	0	0	0	0	0	0	0	0	0	0	0	.233	.270	.292	1	3b
08/17/54	2	AT CHI N	0	1	0	0	0	0	0	0	0	0	0	0	0	0	0	0	0	.232	.269	.290	9	ph
08/22/54		AT STL N	0	1	0	0	0	0	0	0	0	0	0	0	0	0	0	0	0	.231	.268	.289	9	ph,3b
08/29/54	2	VS PHI N	1	4	1	3	0	0	0	3	1	0	0	0	0	0	0	1	0	.240	.278	.305	1	3b
08/30/54		VS PHI N	1	5	0	0	0	0	0	0	0	0	0	0	0	0	0	0	0	.235	.273	.299	1	3b
08/31/54		VS PHI N	0	1	0	0	0	0	0	0	0	0	0	0	0	0	0	0	0	.234	.272	.298	9	ph
09/03/54		VS MIL N	0	1	0	0	0	0	0	0	0	0	0	0	0	0	0	0	0	.233	.271	.296	9	ph
09/04/54		VS MIL N	0	1	0	0	0	0	0	0	1	0	0	0	0	0	0	0	0	.232	.270	.295	9	ph
09/05/54	1	VS MIL N	0	1	0	0	0	0	0	0	0	0	0	0	0	0	0	0	0	.231	.269	.294	9	ph
09/05/54	2	VS MIL N	1	5	1	2	0	0	0	0	0	0	0	0	0	0	0	1	0	.235	.271	.296	1	3b
09/06/54		VS STL N	1	4	0	1	0	0	0	0	0	0	0	0	0	0	0	0	0	.235	.270	.295	1	3b
09/08/54		AT PHI N	1	4	2	3	0	0	0	0	0	0	1	0	0	0	0	1	0	.243	.279	.302	1	3b
09/11/54		AT NY N	1	3	1	1	0	0	0	0	0	0	1	0	1	0	0	0	0	.244	.280	.314	1	3b
09/12/54	2	AT PIT N	1	4	2	1	0	0	0	0	1	0	0	0	0	0	0	0	0	.244	.282	.313	1	3b
09/13/54		AT PIT N	1	5	0	0	0	0	0	0	0	0	1	0	0	0	0	0	0	.239	.277	.307	1	3b
09/14/54		AT BRO N	0	1	0	0	0	0	0	0	0	0	0	0	0	0	0	0	0	.238	.276	.306	9	ph
09/19/54		VS CHI N	0	1	0	0	0	0	0	0	0	0	0	0	0	0	0	0	0	.238	.275	.305	9	ph,3b
09/20/54	1	AT MIL N	1	4	0	1	0	0	0	0	1	0	0	0	0	0	0	0	0	.238	.277	.304	1	3b

Special Notes and Documents

Emancipation Proclamation

By the President of the United States of America: A Proclamation.
September 22, 1862

Whereas, on the twenty-second day of September, in the year of our Lord one thousand eight hundred and sixty-two, a proclamation was issued by the President of the United States, containing, among other things, the following, to wit:

That on the first day of January, in the year of our Lord one thousand eight hundred and sixty-three, all persons held as slaves within any State or designated part of a State, the people whereof shall then be in rebellion against the United States, shall be then, thenceforward, and forever free; and the Executive Government of the United States, including the military and naval authority thereof, will recognize and maintain the freedom of such persons, and will do no act or acts to repress such persons, or any of them, in any efforts they may make for their actual freedom.

That the Executive will, on the first day of January aforesaid, by proclamation, designate the States and parts of States, if any, in which the people thereof, respectively, shall then be in rebellion against the United

States; and the fact that any State, or the people thereof, shall on that day be, in good faith, represented in the Congress of the United States by members chosen thereto at elections wherein a majority of the qualified voters of such State shall have participated, shall, in the absence of strong countervailing testimony, be deemed conclusive evidence that such State, and the people thereof, are not then in rebellion against the United States.

Now, therefore I, Abraham Lincoln, President of the United States, by virtue of the power in me vested as Commander-in-Chief, of the Army and Navy of the United States in time of actual armed rebellion against the authority and government of the United States, and as a fit and necessary war measure for suppressing said rebellion, do, on this first day of January, in the year of our Lord one thousand eight hundred and sixty-three, and in accordance with my purpose so to do publicly proclaimed for the full period of one hundred days, from the day first above mentioned, order and designate as the States and parts of States wherein the people thereof respectively, are this day in rebellion against the United States, the following, to wit:

Arkansas, Texas, Louisiana, (except the Parishes of St. Bernard, Plaquemines, Jefferson, St. John, St. Charles, St. James Ascension, Assumption, Terrebonne, Lafourche, St. Mary, St. Martin, and Orleans, including the City of New Orleans) Mississippi, Alabama, Florida, Georgia, South Carolina, North Carolina, and Virginia, (except the forty-eight counties designated as West Virginia, and also the counties of Berkley, Accomack, Northampton, Elizabeth City, York, Princess Ann, and Norfolk, including the cities of Norfolk and Portsmouth[)], and which excepted parts, are for the present, left precisely as if this proclamation were not issued.

And by virtue of the power, and for the purpose aforesaid, I do order and declare that all persons held as slaves within said designated States, and parts of States, are, and henceforward shall be free; and that the Executive government of the United States, including the military and naval authorities thereof, will recognize and maintain the freedom of said persons.

And I hereby enjoin upon the people so declared to be free to abstain from all violence, unless in necessary self-defense; and I recommend to them that, in all cases when allowed, they labor faithfully for reasonable wages.

And I further declare and make known, that such persons of suitable condition, will be received into the armed service of the United States to garrison forts, positions, stations, and other places, and to man vessels of all sorts in said service.

And upon this act, sincerely believed to be an act of justice, warranted by the Constitution, upon military necessity, I invoke the considerate judgment of mankind, and the gracious favor of Almighty God.

In witness whereof, I have hereunto set my hand and caused the seal of the United States to be affixed.

Done at the City of Washington, this first day of January, in the year of our Lord one thousand eight hundred and sixty three, and of the Independence of the United States of America the eighty-seventh.

By the President: Abraham Lincoln
William H. Seward, Secretary of State.

President John F. Kennedy's Civil Rights Address

June 11, 1963

Good evening, my fellow citizens.

This afternoon, following a series of threats and defiant statements, the presence of Alabama National Guardsmen was required on the University of Alabama to carry out the final and unequivocal order of the United States District Court of the Northern District of Alabama. That order called for the admission of two clearly qualified young Alabama residents who happened to have been born Negro. That they were admitted peacefully on the campus is due in good measure to the conduct of the students of the University of Alabama, who met their responsibilities in a constructive way.

I hope that every American, regardless of where he lives, will stop and examine his conscience about this and other related incidents. This Nation was founded by men of many nations and backgrounds. It was founded on the principle that all men are created equal, and that the rights of every man are diminished when the rights of one man are threatened.

Today, we are committed to a worldwide struggle to promote and protect the rights of all who wish to be free. And when Americans are sent to Vietnam or West Berlin, we do not ask for Whites only. It ought to be possible, therefore, for American students of any color to attend any public institution they select without having to be backed up by troops. It ought to be possible for American consumers of any color to receive equal service in places of public accommodation, such as hotels and restaurants and theaters and retail stores, without being forced to resort to demonstrations in the street, and it ought to be possible for American citizens of any color to register and to vote in a free election without interference or fear of reprisal. It ought to be possible, in short, for every American to enjoy the privileges of being American without regard to his race or his color. In short, every American ought to have the right to be treated as he would wish to be treated, as one would wish his children to be treated. But this is not the case.

The Negro baby born in America today, regardless of the section of the State in which he is born, has about one-half as much chance of completing a high school as a White baby born in the same place on the same day, one-third as much chance of completing college, one-third as much chance of becoming a professional man, twice as much chance of becoming unemployed, about one-seventh as much chance of earning $10,000 a year, a life expectancy which is 7 years shorter, and the prospects of earning only half as much.

This is not a sectional issue. Difficulties over segregation and discrimination exist in every city, in every State of the Union, producing in many cities a rising tide of discontent that threatens the public safety. Nor is this a partisan issue. In a time of domestic crisis men of good will and generosity should be able to unite regardless of party or politics. This is not even a legal or legislative issue alone. It is better to settle these matters in the courts than on the streets, and new laws are needed at every level, but law alone cannot make men see right. We are confronted primarily with a moral issue. It is as old as the Scriptures and is as clear as the American Constitution.

The heart of the question is whether all Americans are to be afforded equal rights and equal opportunities, whether we are going to treat our fellow Americans as we want to be treated. If an American, because his skin is dark, cannot eat lunch in a restaurant open to the public, if he cannot send his children to the best public school available, if he cannot vote for the public officials who will represent him, if, in short, he cannot enjoy the full and free life which all of us want, then who among us would be content to have the color of his skin changed and stand in his place? Who among us would then be content with the counsels of patience and delay?

One hundred years of delay have passed since President Lincoln freed the slaves, yet their heirs, their grandsons, are not fully free. They are not yet freed from the bonds of injustice. They are not yet freed from social and economic oppression. And this Nation, for all its hopes and all its boasts, will not be fully free until all its citizens are free.

We preach freedom around the world, and we mean it, and we cherish our freedom here at home, but are we to say to the world, and much more importantly, to each other that this is the land of the free except for the Negroes; that we have no second-class citizens except Negroes; that we have no class or caste system, no ghettoes, no master race except with respect to Negroes?

169

Now the time has come for this Nation to fulfill its promise. The events in Birmingham and elsewhere have so increased the cries for equality that no city or State or legislative body can prudently choose to ignore them. The fires of frustration and discord are burning in every city, North and South, where legal remedies are not at hand. Redress is sought in the streets, in demonstrations, parades, and protests which create tensions and threaten violence and threaten lives.

We face, therefore, a moral crisis as a country and a people. It cannot be met by repressive police action. It cannot be left to increased demonstrations in the streets. It cannot be quieted by token moves or talk. It is a time to act in the Congress, in your State and local legislative body and, above all, in all of our daily lives. It is not enough to pin the blame on others, to say this a problem of one section of the country or another, or deplore the facts that we face. A great change is at hand, and our task, our obligation, is to make that revolution, that change, peaceful and constructive for all. Those who do nothing are inviting shame, as well as violence. Those who act boldly are recognizing right, as well as reality.

Next week I shall ask the Congress of the United States to act, to make a commitment it has not fully made in this century to the proposition that race has no place in American life or law. The Federal judiciary has upheld that proposition in a series of forthright cases. The Executive Branch has adopted that proposition in the conduct of its affairs, including the employment of Federal personnel, the use of Federal facilities, and the sale of federally financed housing. But there are other necessary measures which only the Congress can provide, and they must be provided at this session. The old code of equity law under which we live commands for every wrong a remedy, but in too many communities, in too many parts of the country, wrongs are inflicted on Negro citizens and there are no remedies at law. Unless the Congress acts, their only remedy is the street.

I am, therefore, asking the Congress to enact legislation giving all Americans the right to be served in facilities which are open to the public—hotels, restaurants, theaters, retail stores, and similar establishments. This seems to me to be an elementary right. Its denial is an arbitrary indignity that no American in 1963 should have to endure, but many do.

I have recently met with scores of business leaders urging them to take voluntary action to end this discrimination, and I have been encouraged by their response, and in the last two weeks over 75 cities have seen progress made in desegregating these kinds of facilities. But many are unwilling to act alone, and for this reason, nationwide legislation is needed if we are to move this problem from the streets to the courts.

I'm also asking the Congress to authorize the Federal Government to participate more fully in lawsuits designed to end segregation in public education. We have succeeded in persuading many districts to desegregate voluntarily. Dozens have admitted Negroes without violence. Today, a Negro is attending a State-supported institution in every one of our 50 States, but the pace is very slow.

Too many Negro children entering segregated grade schools at the time of the Supreme Court's decision nine years ago will enter segregated high schools this fall, having suffered a loss which can never be restored. The lack of an adequate education denies the Negro a chance to get a decent job.

The orderly implementation of the Supreme Court decision, therefore, cannot be left solely to those who may not have the economic resources to carry the legal action or who may be subject to harassment.

Other features will be also requested, including greater protection for the right to vote. But legislation, I repeat, cannot solve this problem alone. It must be solved in the homes of every American in every community across our country. In this respect I want to pay tribute to those citizens North and South who've been working in their communities to make life better for all. They are acting not out of sense of legal duty but out of a sense of human decency. Like our soldiers and sailors in all parts of the world they are meeting freedom's challenge on the firing line, and I salute them for their honor and their courage.

My fellow Americans, this is a problem which faces us all—in every city of the North as well as the South. Today, there are Negroes unemployed, two or three times as many compared to Whites, inadequate education, moving into the large cities, unable to find work, young people particularly out of work without hope, denied equal rights, denied the opportunity to eat at a restaurant or a lunch counter or go to a movie theater, denied the right to a decent education, denied almost today the right to attend a State university even though qualified. It seems to me that these are matters which concern us all, not merely Presidents or Congressmen or Governors, but every citizen of the United States.

This is one country. It has become one country because all of us and all the people who came here had an equal chance to develop their talents. We cannot say to ten percent of the population that you can't have that right; that your children cannot have the chance to develop whatever talents they have; that the only way that they are going to get their rights is to go in the street and demonstrate. I think we owe them and we owe ourselves a better country than that.

Therefore, I'm asking for your help in making it easier for us to move ahead and to provide the kind of equality of treatment which we would want ourselves; to give a chance for every child to be educated to the limit of his talents.

As I've said before, not every child has an equal talent or an equal ability or equal motivation, but they should have the equal right to develop their talent and their ability and their motivation, to make something of themselves.

We have a right to expect that the Negro community will be responsible, will uphold the law, but they have a right to expect that the law will be fair, that the Constitution will be color blind, as Justice Harlan said at the turn of the century.

This is what we're talking about and this is a matter which concerns this country and what it stands for, and in meeting it I ask the support of all our citizens.

Thank you very much.

The "I Have a Dream" Speech

Martin Luther King, Jr.
August 28, 1963

I am happy to join with you today in what will go down in history as the greatest demonstration for freedom in the history of our nation.

Five score years ago, a great American, in whose symbolic shadow we stand today, signed the Emancipation Proclamation. This momentous decree came as a great beacon light of hope to millions of Negro slaves who had been seared in the flames of withering injustice. It came as a joyous daybreak to end the long night of their captivity.

But one hundred years later, the Negro still is not free. One hundred years later, the life of the Negro is still sadly crippled by the manacles of segregation and the chains of discrimination. One hundred years later, the Negro lives on a lonely island of poverty in the midst of a vast ocean of material prosperity. One hundred years later, the Negro is still languished in the corners of American society and finds himself an exile in his own land. And so we've come here today to dramatize a shameful condition.

In a sense we've come to our nation's capital to cash a check. When the architects of our republic wrote the magnificent words of the Constitution and the Declaration of Independence, they were signing a promissory note to which every American was to fall heir. This note was a promise that all men, yes, Black men as well as White men, would be guaranteed the "unalienable Rights" of "Life, Liberty and the pursuit of Happiness." It is obvious today that America has defaulted on this promissory note, insofar as her citizens of color are concerned. Instead of honoring this sacred obligation, America has given the Negro people a bad check, a check which has come back marked "insufficient funds."

But we refuse to believe that the bank of justice is bankrupt. We refuse to believe that there are insufficient funds in the great vaults of opportunity of this nation. And so, we've come to cash this check, a check that will give us upon demand the riches of freedom and the security of justice.

We have also come to this hallowed spot to remind America of the fierce urgency of Now. This is no time to engage in the luxury of cooling off or to take the tranquilizing drug of gradualism. Now is the time to make real the promises of democracy. Now is the time to rise from the dark and desolate valley of segregation to the sunlit path of racial justice. Now is the time to lift our nation from the quicksands of racial injustice to the solid rock of brotherhood. Now is the time to make justice a reality for all of God's children.

It would be fatal for the nation to overlook the urgency of the moment. This sweltering summer of the Negro's legitimate discontent will not pass until there is an invigorating autumn of freedom and equality. Nineteen sixty-three is not an end, but a beginning. And those who hope that the Negro needed to blow off steam and will now be content will have a rude awakening if the nation returns to business as usual. And there will be neither rest nor tranquility in America until the Negro is granted his citizenship rights. The whirlwinds of revolt will continue to shake the foundations of our nation until the bright day of justice emerges.

But there is something that I must say to my people, who stand on the warm threshold which leads into the palace of justice: In the process of gaining our rightful place, we must not be guilty of wrongful deeds. Let us not seek to satisfy our thirst for freedom by drinking from the cup of bitterness and hatred. We must forever conduct our struggle on the high plane of dignity and discipline. We must not allow our creative protest to degenerate into physical violence. Again and again, we must rise to the majestic heights of meeting physical force with soul force.

The marvelous new militancy which has engulfed the Negro community must not lead us to a distrust of all White people, for many of our White brothers, as evidenced by their presence here today, have come to realize that their destiny is tied up with our destiny. And they have come to realize that their freedom is inextricably bound to our freedom.

We cannot walk alone.

And as we walk, we must make the pledge that we shall always march ahead.

We cannot turn back.

There are those who are asking the devotees of civil rights, "When will you be satisfied?" We can never be satisfied as long as the Negro is the victim of the unspeakable horrors of police brutality. We can never be satisfied as long as our bodies, heavy with the fatigue of travel, cannot gain lodging in the motels of the highways and the hotels of the cities. We cannot be satisfied as long as the Negro's basic mobility is from a smaller ghetto to a larger one. We can never be satisfied as long as our children are stripped of their self-hood and robbed of their dignity by signs stating: "For Whites Only." We cannot be satisfied as long as a Negro in Mississippi cannot vote and a Negro in New York believes he has nothing for which to vote. No, no, we are not satisfied, and we will not be satisfied until "justice rolls down like waters, and righteousness like a mighty stream."

I am not unmindful that some of you have come here out of great trials and tribulations. Some of you have come fresh from narrow jail cells. And some of you have come from areas where your quest -- quest for freedom left you battered by the storms of persecution and staggered by the winds of police brutality. You have been the veterans of creative suffering. Continue to work with the faith that unearned suffering is redemptive. Go back to Mississippi, go back to Alabama, go back to South Carolina, go back to Georgia, go back to Louisiana, go back to the slums and ghettos of our northern cities, knowing that somehow this situation can and will be changed.

Let us not wallow in the valley of despair, I say to you today, my friends.

And so even though we face the difficulties of today and tomorrow, I still have a dream. It is a dream deeply rooted in the American dream.

I have a dream that one day this nation will rise up and live out the true meaning of its creed: "We hold these truths to be self-evident, that all men are created equal."

I have a dream that one day on the red hills of Georgia, the sons of former slaves and the sons of former slave owners will be able to sit down together at the table of brotherhood.

I have a dream that one day even the state of Mississippi, a state sweltering with the heat of injustice, sweltering with the heat of oppression, will be transformed into an oasis of freedom and justice.

I have a dream that my four little children will one day live in a nation where they will not be judged by the color of their skin but by the content of their character.

I have a *dream* today!

I have a dream that one day, down in Alabama, with its vicious racists, with its governor having his lips dripping with the words of "interposition" and "nullification"—one day right there in Alabama little Black boys and Black girls will be able to join hands with little White boys and White girls as sisters and brothers.

I have a *dream* today!

I have a dream that one day every valley shall be exalted, and every hill and mountain shall be made low, the rough places will be made plain, and the crooked places will be made straight; "and the glory of the Lord shall be revealed and all flesh shall see it together."

This is our hope, and this is the faith that I go back to the South with.

With this faith, we will be able to hew out of the mountain of despair a stone of hope. With this faith, we will be able to transform the jangling discords of our nation into a beautiful symphony of brotherhood. With this faith, we will be able to work together, to pray together, to struggle together, to go to jail together, to stand up for freedom together, knowing that we will be free one day.

And this will be the day—this will be the day when all of God's children will be able to sing with new meaning:

My country 'tis of thee, sweet land of liberty, of thee I sing.
Land where my fathers died, land of the Pilgrim's pride,
From every mountainside, let freedom ring!

And if America is to be a great nation, this must become true.

And so let freedom ring from the prodigious hilltops of New Hampshire.

Let freedom ring from the mighty mountains of New York.

Let freedom ring from the heightening Alleghenies of Pennsylvania.

Let freedom ring from the snow-capped Rockies of Colorado.

Let freedom ring from the curvaceous slopes of California.

But not only that:

Let freedom ring from Stone Mountain of Georgia.

Let freedom ring from Lookout Mountain of Tennessee.

Let freedom ring from every hill and molehill of Mississippi.

From every mountainside, let freedom ring.

And when this happens, when we allow freedom ring, when we let it ring from every village and every hamlet, from every state and every city, we will be able to speed up that day when *all* of God's children, Black men and White men, Jews and Gentiles, Protestants and Catholics, will be able to join hands and sing in the words of the old Negro spiritual:

Free at last! Free at last!

Thank God Almighty, we are free at last!

References and Resources

Abraham Lincoln Presidential Library
Associated Press
Baseballprospectus.com
Baseballreference.com
Bill Hornaday
Bill Reinberger
Bradley, Leo. *Underrated Reds*, 2009
Cheryl Harmon
Chuck Harmon Jr.
Cincinnati Commercial-Gazette
Cincinnati Enquirer
Cincinnati Historical Society Library
Cincinnati Museum Center
Cincinnati Post
Cincinnati Reds
Cincinnati Reds Hall of Fame
Cincinnati Times-Star
Courtis Fuller
Dr. Martin Luther King, Jr, Library
Eig, Jonathan. *Opening Day, The Story of Jackie Robinson's First Season*, 2007
Flood, Curt. *The Way It Is*, 1972
Gary Robbins
Gene Miller
George Vogel

The (Gloversville) Leader-Republican

Herb Schowmeyer

Hirsch, James S. *Willie Mays, The Life, The Legend*, 2010

Indiana High School Athletic Association

Indiana High School Baseball Hall of Fame

Indiana High School Basketball Hall of Fame

Indiana State Museum

Indiana University Herman B Wells Library

Indiana University School of Journalism

Indiana University National Sports Journalism Center

Indianapolis Newspapers, Inc. *Indiana High School Basketball Tournament Record Book*, 1990, 1995

Jacobson, Steve. *Carrying Jackie's Torch*, 2007

Jarrod Rollins

John F. Kennedy Presidential Library and Museum

Kelley, Brent. *Voices from the Negro League,*

Kit Klingelhoffer

Lawson, Earl. *Cincinnati Seasons*, 1987

Lorri Zeller

Los Angeles Dodgers, Josh Rawitch

Major League Baseball

Mike Myers

Mitchell Potts

MLB.com

McClure, Rusty, with David Stern and Michael Banks. *Crosley*, 2007

NAACP of Cincinnati

National Underground Railroad Freedom Center

Negro League Baseball Museum

Pete Rose

Philadelphia Phillies

Pittsburgh Post-Gazette

Rampersad, Arnold. *Jackie Robinson, a Biography*, 1997

Retrosheet.org

Rhodes, Greg, and John Erardi. *Big Red Dynasty*, 1997

Rhodes, Greg, and John Erardi. *Crosley Fields*, 1995

Rhodes, Greg. *Cincinnati Reds Hall of Fame Highlights*, 2007

Rhodes, Greg, and John Erardi. *The First Boys of Summer*, 1994

Rhodes, Greg, and John Snyder. *Redleg Journal*, 2000

Riley, James A. *The Biographical Encyclopedia of the Negro Baseball Leagues*, 1994

Robert Padgett, www.hatchets.net

Shannon, Mike. *More Tales from the Dugout*

Simon, Scott. *Jackie Robinson and the Integration of Baseball*, 2002

St. Louis Cardinals

The Baseball Almanac

The Baseball Chronicle

The New York Times

Washington (Indiana) Times-Herald

The Columbia Club of Indianapolis

Time Magazine, July 1955

Time.com/time/magazine/article/0.9171

Tony Williams

Tye, Larry. *Satchel, The Life and Times of an American Legend*, 2009

WLWT Television, Channel 5, Cincinnati

Ward, Geoffrey C., and Ken Burns. *Baseball, an Illustrated History*, 1994

Washington High School

Wikipedia.org

Williams, Pat, with Mike Sielski. *How to Be Like Jackie Robinson*, 2004

WJCP Radio 1460 AM North Vernon, Indiana. wjcpradio.com

ABOUT THE AUTHOR

Marty Pieratt is an Emmy-Award winning television reporter who has also worked in newspapers, radio, and public relations. He owned and operated seven radio stations in Kentucky and Indiana. He is a visiting professor at the Indiana University School of Journalism at Bloomington. This is his third book.

Marty Pieratt may be contacted at
martypieratt@yahoo.com or www.martypieratt.com